EXLIBRIS

Common-Sense
Guide to
REFINISHING
ANTIQUES

Common-Sense Guide to REFINISHING ANTIQUES

New, Enlarged Edition

by Alfred Higgins

A Funk & Wagnalls Book
Published by Thomas Y. Crowell
New York

Manufactured in the United States of America

Library of Congress Cataloging in Publication Data

Higgins, Alfred, 1906-
　Common-sense guide to refinishing antiques.
　Includes index.
　1. Furniture finishing. I. Title.
TT199.4H53　1976　　　684.1'0443　　　76-8913
ISBN 0-308-10252-5
　2 3 4 5 6 7 8 9 10

DEDICATED *to the designers and craftsmen of the past whose creations have such charm and warmth and to the men and women of today who are faithfully preserving the old furnishings recaptured from attics, barns, and acquired at auctions and shops along the wayside.*

FOREWORD

Whether you collect antiques for pleasure or profit, spend a little or a lot, the pursuit can be tremendously rewarding. The styles and fine craftsmanship of the past enhance any home, provide comfort, and create a friendly atmosphere for family and friends alike. Antiques convey a sense of human warmth in a way that brand-new pieces cannot possibly match until they, too, have been seasoned by daily use.

Building a collection of antiques is at once a lifelong task and an achievement that will never fade away. For me, the greatest thrill is not so much in finding beautiful pieces, though that is always exciting, but in spotting a saddened, time-worn chair or table—something that can be purchased for a song—and then restoring it to its original condition. Through the process of restoration, I exercise my mind and hand, while at the same time refreshing my soul, as I see the piece gradually reacquire the characteristics of beauty and usefulness imparted to it by the original maker. In a real sense, the piece lives again, once more to cheer the eye and fulfill its function.

Restoration and refinishing, then, are the subjects of this book. Herein lies the real joy of antiquing. Through restoration and refinishing, you can express your personality and your ability, while at the same time, giving your home the distinctive vitality that comes from having handmade furniture, which has been mellowed through use, cherished over the years, and renewed with loving care. As you devote more time to restoring and refinishing, you will not only benefit therapeutically in mind and body but automatically gain new "friends" that will comfort you in future years.

This book explains in simple form the techniques of restoration and refinishing that provide the best results in terms of endurance as well as immediate appearance; it dispenses with mystical, all-too-often mystifying procedures in favor of good old-fashioned common sense. All the rules herein are trustworthy, the fruit of forty years of searching and testing. It is a safe road that I have marked out; travel on it and you should experience no dangers, no failures.

My hope is that you will find as much enjoyment from restoration and refinishing as I have—and that your home will be graced as a result, with as many handsome antiques as you wish to put in it.

CONTENTS

A picture-direction section showing
in detail what to do and how to do it.

PART *I*

Antiques to Refinish

1. WHAT IS AN ANTIQUE?

Inasmuch as we are primarily concerned with durable and usable old furniture or home furnishings that are of a pleasing, practical, and interesting design, there should be some interpretation of the word "antique." We know, perhaps, that much of the furniture referred to by that term stems from the right tree but perhaps not from the richest branch. In certain places antique means old, or a copy of the old, but not necessarily "original," or "priceless," or "one-of-a-kind."

The word antique is given a broad interpretation throughout the world. It takes on many different meanings and often it depends upon where you are and with whom you are traveling what interpretation it may have. We read roadsigns that simply say *Antiques,* but the shops may contain antiquities of great rarity and value or they may be filled with junk. The chances are much better that they are stocked with choice secondhand pieces at a low or reasonable cost. If you can accept those scratches, mars, dents, and bruises, and if the piece is also in restorable condition, by following this book's shop methods of refinishing (and allowing yourself some tolerance in the meaning of "antique") you will possess antiques—and you will be able to have them at the lowest cost. Besides, you will feel much more as if they are truly yours for having had a hand in their restoration.

Pursuing the Definition

By one authoritative definition, a person is an antique if he belongs to the older generation and is still visible. A broader definition is that an antique is merely something old—so it looks as if the certainty of age must be our beginning point before we can reach a conclusion. How about an egg? If it has been forgotten in the henhouse for six months. . . . How about last year's fresh blueberries? Now you begin to see that age alone is not the criterion. The antique automobile fanciers specify that an automobile rolls into that category exactly on its twenty-fifth birthday. But, we ask again, are such automobiles relics of the past that have charm, beauty, or real use?

If "antique" means merely the number of years, then how many years must it be for furniture? What do the "experts" say? One curator claims that furniture must have been manufactured more than one hundred years ago. Another states that he likes "thirty years of being" for the designation. Until recently the United States Customs Bureau classified as antiques only those household articles manufactured before 1830. Canada chose the date of 1847, while Great Britain maintains the one-hundred-year-old standard. At this point perhaps you think the definition could lead to an international dispute. Let us try once more.

One good reference states that an antique must be old, esthetic, historic, and have financial value. That gives us something solid to put our feet on. We know that some things get nicer and more mellow as they get older and as something from the past begins to stand alone—ah, now we have our own definition!

An antique is something that has survived most of its brothers and sisters and, by the temper of its time and the personality of the maker, carries over to us that desirable character and charm which makes it worthy of admission to the company of revered elders.

Does that satisfy you as a definition? Some people are inclined to think of antiques as something sad, wornout, and dirty. But if a saw has lost its teeth, is that antiquity or someone's stupidity? It would more likely be a sign of improper metal dentistry or a poor wood diet. If someone spills a bottle of ink over a table, is that antiquing? If someone never bothers to houseclean, is that antiquing? We must let common sense be our guide, our own good taste and preferences, and our knowledge and experience lead us to the real values. There are true antiques and there are many reproductions of varying age. Whatever offers you comfort and delight can be your "antique." Go confidently on your way and let this book dull the trials and insulate you from the troubles so that you will have fun on your antiquing journeys.

If you will adopt the methods of easy refinishing and restoring given here, the senseless complications and technicalities will melt before your eyes.

Antiques and Reproductions

When you are antiquing, you will be told time and again, "This is not a reproduction, it is an original." This may or may not be true, depending on the integrity of the dealer. But ask yourself these questions: Who has reproductions and who has originals? How many originals are available? What is an original?

In the shops of the great designers and makers of furniture, all the pieces that came out were originals because the

maker had a hand in their creation. Even so, many of the
pieces were more or less exact copies of an original design so
that the term "original" is already a little fuzzy. As an
example of how elastic this term is, and how little it may
have to do with true age, consider the Shaker chairs. These
were made originally in the 1700s and sold across the
northeastern states by itinerant Shaker peddlers in order to
gain a livelihood for their colony. But as recently as 1920 I
lived next door to two of these religious colonies and actually
witnessed the making of the slim, well-formed Shaker chairs.
Made from the original pattern, they were authentic Shaker
pieces because Shakers made them and today it is not
impossible to locate some of these "originals," these recently-

A MIXTURE OF GOOD WALNUT AND MAHOGANY PICKED UP
FOR A SONG

Or, in some instances they may be had for nothing, such was
the case of the large tip-top table that was missing one leg. The
base of the tip-top table was walnut, so I searched for a piece of
walnut and cut out a new leg with a saber saw. Matching the two
remaining legs was not difficult with the use of various sanding
papers and matching stains. No one can tell for sure which is the
new leg.

The small candle-stand top had part of the raised lip broken
away. A stiff mix of very fine sawdust and epoxy glue was molded
with the fingers in the break, for a slightly mounded fill, and
allowed to dry for three days. Then emery papers were used to
cut the fill to proper shape and size. With a preliminary tint of
stain on the fill and a full staining over the whole piece, the
finishing coats of varnish and a hard wax polishing brought about
a complete rejuvenation.

The Martha Washington sewing cabinet was scratched and the
old finish marred. Stripping and refinishing put it back into full
bloom again, its fine woods sparkling with a clear-grained finish.

made "antiques." But what happens to the one-hundred-year's stipulation?

All furniture made in the seventeenth and eighteenth centuries, and that produced in the early part of the nineteenth century, can safely be classified as "antique"; if it was made by a craftsman but not reproduced by a factory it may even be an "original." But most of the furniture made since then has to be reproductions: makers copied or adapted the styles of William and Mary, Queen Anne, Chippendale, Hepplewhite, Duncan Phyfe, Sheraton, Empire, the French Louis', and the later Victorian, Mission, Grand Rapids, or whatever other designation might be applied. There are two groups of furniture that do not have an aristocratic background, and from these unheralded cabinet-making sources we get most of our "originals" in this country, which are our native "antiques." We refer to that furniture which was handcrafted by the early settlers and to that which was made in the shops on the lands of back-country gentlemen. These pieces are sound, firm, and usually practical, but in the case of the settlers' furniture particularly, a little on the crude side. We call this furniture "primitive" and it may come pretty close to being the surest kind of antique. Many American farmers made their own furniture and also gave away or sold pieces to relatives and friends. In the winter, in sheds and shops, they sawed and carved and made things that would last. The more sophisticated pieces aped the furniture of the cities made by more adept craftsmen, adapting the more elaborate designs. Fullness of proportion, solidity, and the choicest native woods characterize this furniture which was put together with great care and cleverness. We call this "country" furniture today and the manufacturers are now reproducing many features developed by farm craftsmen.

In general, reproductions are faithful copies of the original piece. Often the same kind of wood is used and the better designed pieces are taken as the source. Today you may find, if you are lucky, excellent cabinetmakers who survive in our scientific era and it is not impossible to locate a third-, fourth-, or even a sixth-generation chairmaker, still reproducing designs faithfully. Sometimes it is possible to purchase such pieces in the unfinished condition and save money. You will find the finishing procedures outlined in this book helpful for these. And helpful also for furniture purchased in a "knocked-down" kit that you put together and finish yourself. Such work is fun and your grandchildren will enjoy having your "antiques" even if they are not originals in the true sense. Before buying such kits or unfinished furniture, double check on the kind and condition of the woods and that adequate information is given about how to put pieces together. If the style is "Colonial," make sure that the wood fits the time—maple and pine were the woods used most frequently. Some other things to check are that the maker has seasoned or cured the wood for two to three years before cutting it, thus avoiding warping, shrinkage, and splits later on. Mortise-and-tenon joints, dowels and dovetails, tongue and groove are all signs of good craftsmanship. Nails, slots, or housed joints and half-track tongue and groove (called "rabbeting"), are all signs of shoddy work which is never a bargain. Before you purchase new reproductions to finish, be sure to consult the sections of this book on smoothing, staining, and finishing.

If you do not enjoy searching for antiques, that hobby of "antiquing" so many pursue, you can buy these reproductions and enjoy their beauty, taking pleasure in your contribution to the finished product. The world is full of antiques and reproductions and as good butterfly tables are available in our day as were made in 1700—so far as design, construction, and use are concerned. But if you want to search out the unusual, if you take pleasure in the pursuit as well as in the possession, then you are a real "antiquer" and you will want to know more about where to go, what to look for, and how to be sure what you buy has true worth.

2. BECOMING AN ANTIQUER

Visit Collections of Antiques

To gain additional understanding and improve your working knowledge of what to look for in antiques and how they are used, visit the many museums and collections, particularly the restored homes and the historic houses open to the public where you can see fine furniture of the past. There, carefully preserved and displayed, you will see furniture and household fittings arranged in surroundings as authentically restored as research and records can produce. Many millions of dollars and many hours of scholarly research have gone into making these repositories of the past correct in every detail. You may find pieces there which, if they could be auctioned today, would bring hundreds, or in some cases thousands of dollars. Original pieces, some of them unique, are indeed priceless today.

You will be sure to notice, with your heightened interest in refinishing antiques, that many pieces have not been touched or that they have been only slightly retouched. Their surface conditions may be considered poor or bad by most refinishers. There are practical reasons why they are thus, but these reasons will not apply to most of our own projects. First, if the old finish were removed and new finishes applied, even the experts would be more confused than they are on occasion today. Second, it is good to see some things as near as possible to the condition in which they were used by our forefathers. Third, the article is now out of use by humans and can safely be shown unrenovated.

As I have suggested elsewhere, unless you are reasonably sure that your piece is an original masterpiece, do not have any compunction about refinishing and reclaiming it so that it can be put back into good-as-new working order, or as near to it as you can achieve. Make it clean, bright, and "healthy" so that you can cherish it—and *use* it. By doing this, you may be preserving furniture so that it will last another hundred or two hundred years to delight future generations. Your antiques may be somewhat younger than those we are permitted to view in museums and in restorations of old houses but they will live as long in the end and perhaps be more useful. Because your pieces should be useful, the whole aspect will be different from that of a museum. You will be choosing for use, which will govern your choice and narrow it, while a museum chooses for authenticity and correctness, whether or not the pieces would fit into our lives today. The fact that Lafayette slept in a particular bed is today less important to us than the crucial fact of its comfort as a modern sleeping place. Therefore the modern approach to decorating with antiques has relaxed from the older one of making everything so authentic that one might as well have been living in an eighteenth-century farmhouse with no modern conveniences at all. Just as we would not want to cook over a fireplace or use an oven which had to be heated from a wood fire, so do we now want comfort as well as utility in the antiques we mix with modern pieces or with antiques of more than one particular period.

As you go antiquing you may find old magazines, journals, books, and catalogs that will interest you and give you a certain background for your hobby. Many antique shops have magazines and books printed more than a hundred years ago which can be purchased for moderate sums. Also there are many fine books on the subject of antiques which cover the various facets at length and much more thoroughly than the scope of this book would allow. These can be of great value to you, giving you many aspects and details to look for in your antiquing journeys and shopping expeditions.

But once you have finished this book, you can take the helm and start your explorations. Some of the safest routes for the novice navigator have been charted.

Collection Points for Antiques

What are the sources for antiques, where might they be hidden away? Where are the greatest potential yields, so that the dollars and hours spent are most productive? All that we must do is to mark the roadmaps of the quickest and best routes to the treasure caches. There are, in the main, six different kinds of places that will probably yield the antiques you are looking for. Here is a briefing, so that you will not waste time and will have some conception of what to expect to find before you arrive at any one of them. The six most productive sources are: attics, barns, antique shops, "flea markets," town dumps, and auctions.

ATTICS. Do you still have access to an attic you knew in your childhood? As you played in it on rainy days you probably thought of it as a clutter of junk, as a source of playtime dress-up material. Looked at with grown up eyes, it may be a vault laden with valuables: a creaky little rocker, a lot of hand-carved picture frames, or one laden with gilt ornament holding a tintype in its ornate recesses. Horsehair-upholstered Victorian sofas and chairs, old chests of drawers, little tables with marble tops, or broken pedestals and table tops without a full complement of legs—all of these may be lurking in the dimness of the attic.

If you were a child of the city apartment era, or if your family possessions were cleared out and disposed of long ago, then you may have friends or acquaintances in the country who will let you go to their attics and purchase what meets your needs or pleases your fancy. "Estate Sales" and "Garage Sales" are advertised in the newspapers and are often worth attending to see what is offered. In addition to furniture, you'll often find china, silver, pewter, brass, and copper accessories, kerosene or other oil lamps, boxes of wood and tin, old family albums, painted tin trays, and the stoneware jugs and crocks that were hand thrown and finished. Attics and their contents are well worth exploring.

BARNS.   The family barn or stable is also a rich mine for you to sample. Barns, as you know, were the workshops of the nation in past years, and they automatically became the catchalls when the farm was happily busy and noisy with cows and chickens, horses and pigs, dogs and cats, not to mention inquisitive kids. The lofts that held hay may have become storage places for out-of-date furniture, for buckets, stools, bins, trivets, sadirons, even millstones; and furniture of the cruder sort that is so prized as "country" style today often was retired to the barn when the flossier products of the machine age were installed in the farmhouse. A little simple chemistry and some elbow grease on your part will restore the pieces and give them a rebirth of use. I guarantee that the day they are delivered to your home will be well remembered and a cause for cheers. Good old barns are gradually disappearing from the American landscape, so I suggest you take advantage of the opportunity presented today.

ANTIQUE SHOPS.   I hardly need to mention this source, since you will be aware of them already if you are interested in antiques. But there are antique shops and antique shops. Some are the haven for the finest pieces of the past; these are located in high-rent districts and have prices to match. Others are mere repositories of any and all objects which might even faintly be called antiques. In fact, the second-hand furniture shops may be a good place to look for pieces of good lines and possible antiquity, or at least age. Prices are usually lower in places that do not call themselves antique shops, but your search will be longer and less rewarding. You will come out dusty and dirty from such places, often with nothing at all to show for your hours of poking, lifting, and moving things about.

On the whole, the little antique shops are the best sources; most of the shopkeepers do not refinish or restore, preferring to make their small profit from the sale alone, and allowing the customer to do the follow-up work. These shopkeepers do not have the time to refinish things because they are busy collecting and trading to keep their stock replenished. The higher prices brought by refinished pieces might mean more storage time until they were sold, so they prefer the quicker sale route. Bargains are often to be found, particularly in shops which do not specialize, and sometimes a knowledgeable shopper may find a piece of true worth that the shopkeeper has not appreciated enough to value properly. In the shops of specialists—in metal, glass, furniture of one period or another—you will find shopkeepers whose knowledge is aimed principally at the narrow field in which they can pursue their trade and evaluate their goods with expert knowledge. The main thing in shops such as these is to call by frequently and look over the stock so that you will be sure not to miss the article you want when it comes into the shop. A dividend of shopping this way is getting to know the antique shop owners, the majority of whom are friendly, trustworthy, and extremely helpful. Often I have sensed that these shopkeepers place more value and interest in being helpful to you and in your appreciation of their things than on the possible money profit. They are genuinely good folk to get acquainted with. There are hundreds of good antique shops within the reach of your local roadmap, and going on a trip is made more interesting by stopping along the way to look for particular pieces or just for what may strike your fancy. You will soon find the better places for the furniture you want, for china, glass, metalwork, and bric-a-brac.

Perhaps a personal story will reveal the bargains to be picked up in shopping this way. My wife and I had been searching for a small, reliable old butterfly table and had planned to pay only about $35 since we were low on cash (and knowledge, too, at that time). We did not know that a sudden popularity had caused a jump in the market, some tables fetching as much as $2,000. We went from shop to shop empty-handed, but our innocence and ignorance of the price spurt kept us going and that is why we finally became the proud owners of two little butterfly tables. Both were genuine, but neither was a cabinetmaker's original and therefore not in the $2,000 class. They had both been heavily blobbed with paint and had been placed out in the weather, relegated to holding pots of geraniums—and that is why we were able to find them at our price. It was our luck that they were genuinely old, and that we were able to strip, restore, and finish them with a few years of experience already behind us. We had the good feeling of personal accomplishment as well as the fun and experience of bringing back worthy pieces to use.

FLEA MARKETS.   Now don't begin to worry—everything is sanitary and right out in the open along some clean country roadside. There is probably not a flea in the whole

A BUTTERFLY TABLE IS FOUND AT LAST

Refinish antiques with thoughtful care. If the wood is good old maple, as in the butterfly table, or oak, don't try to make it look like mahogany. It won't. Do the job so that the finish is in the spirit of the time and in character with the material found in the piece. If the wood is inferior and mixed, it may be wiser to paint the piece, choosing a pleasant harmonious color to blend with the old pieces you place with it. Antiquing will also help to make it at home with them. The butterfly-leaf table in the photograph was refinished in the soft golden honey tones that are so right for maple; the little formal lamp stand with the fine carved and fluted legs was refinished in dark mahogany, taking a cue from the original reddish mahogany stain found on the solid mahogany as it was stripped of its finish.

place; it may not even be called a flea market. *Junque Shop, Swap Shop,* or some other name may be on the sign, or sometimes there isn't even a sign out. In growing numbers, however, the flea markets are appearing across the land, and they are probably here to stay. A flea market is usually a gathering of dealers on some rented acreage so that you can shop for all kinds of things in one place, similar to a conventional shopping center or supermarket, but resembling more an old country fair or carnival with the Ferris wheel missing and without the barkers. Each dealer has a specialty—toys, china, silver, glass, furniture, tools, or pictures—and you can wander from one to the other and back again taking advantage of the offerings without the inconvenience of visiting a dozen or more shops. Most of the pieces will be small, since the shopkeepers look more like a Troop of the Truck, or members of the Station Wagon and Tailgate Association than like conventional dealers. But you may find this a real stakeout for bargains, especially in the afternoon as they prepare to close and possibly reduce prices to keep from hauling back their stock to the home base. Don't expect to find pipe organs, antique pianos, or anything much of prime importance—just things of charm, oddity, or genuine worth. Every market has its purpose, so try them all.

The "junque" shops are well named, since most of them offer as wild an assortment of things as anyone could imagine. Mixed in among rusty old iron implements of doubtful use or value will be found amusing or odd objects, pieces of furniture probably bought in job lots and not yet sorted out by owners who are already out buying other odd lots. They are fun to explore and may yield a treasure.

TOWN DUMPS.   Our nation is wonderfully wasteful and you can begin to estimate the enormousness of our industrial program for creating built-in obsolescence if you visit your town dump and wait a few minutes. If you are a fishing enthusiast, you know that you must often wait for hours for your catch. But not at a town dump. Here, within range of a whiff of old stockings, chicken feathers, orange peels, stretched girdles, sneakers, and what not, you may pick up anything from a whole dresser thrown away because one drawer pull is missing to a desk discarded because a drawer is stuck. I have seen scores of fine chairs condemned to the dump for want of glue or one rung, or, in other instances, without any glaring imperfection. In some towns the dump becomes a place to meet interesting people, as they take their trash to discard it and pick over other people's unwanted materials. One man's trash is another man's treasure. Of course, in many places you may have to apply to your Board of Health for information about how to get your dump-picker's license for the season so that you can join the veterans of the battalion of the Early Dump Pickers. It is an honorable approach and you will probably agree that there are riches in the dumps, for they are periodically loaded with yesterday's good taste. The point is to arrive before the Executive Secretary of the Board of Field Management— the man with the match who sets the dump on fire.

Many valuable and irreplaceable items are recovered by the simple procedure of visiting the dump as often as you can, just before the daily fire is set. It is not any dirtier than going down into an abandoned gold mine with a pick and shovel, and the work is a lot more varied. One veteran picker showed me a cabinet he had retrieved. He did not know the exact period or designation for it, but a reliable antique dealer offered him $75 for it. After he refused the offer and refinished it himself, it probably was worth $200 or more. Exercise discrimination—don't overload your workshop with unusable things just because they are available, or you may end up carting them back where they came from. But to the discerning eye, there will be much that is useful and valuable. Incidentally, when "dumping," hands and feet should be well protected and old clothes are mandatory. But if you stay away from the dump, you may miss meeting some of our best people.

AUCTIONS.   The true auction fancier will never forget the pleasant hours or days spent at auctions for they are the most memorable parts of a collector's life. An auction is full of surprises, and it is often a good way to learn what current prices may be. I recall an auction where a chair was sold, uncovered from its years of peace in an old shed. On general appearance most people would have bid $2 or $3 for it if they felt they needed an old knockabout chair. It brought $500 because it was an original Queen Anne chair. The dealer who purchased it knew that he had a buyer and expected to get $900 for it, once it was restored, since it was a genuine antique. A piece of junk to one person is a valuable and rare find to another.

At another auction twelve pieces of glassware were offered and the attending dealers got at bargain prices what was probably worth $800. It was first-class Pomona glass, rare enough to be valuable, but the public thought it could be duplicated in any department store's housewares and china department. At an auction you have to have some idea not only of what you are looking for, but also of what you are looking at. Join the fray and auctions will help to put a polish on your lengthening intelligence. Make a bid once in a while and become seasoned. On upholstered pieces don't think only of silent springs and quality of upholstery. The framework is far more important. Try to get to the auction early, or if the merchandise is displayed for a few days before the actual sale, visit it and examine things at your leisure. Make notes of what you think you want and set some sort of tentative ceiling on what the value may be to you. Auctioneers are good fellows and so are their staff. Many are walking historians and encyclopedias of trivia as well as worthwhile knowledge. They are good-natured showmen, following a strict code of ethics. Once in a while they can be fooled, but not often. And the better auctions are instructive as well as fun. Here are a few suggestions about how to profit from an auction.

Aside from getting there early to examine the stock, wander about with eyes wide open, then stop roaming and take time to examine carefully whatever you have spotted as being of interest to you. Evaluate its condition, probable age, desirability for use at home, and most of all how transportable it may be. You will probably have to haul it yourself in your car or pay a lot to have it delivered by truck. Next, pick a good position where you can see well and be seen by the auctioneer. If you have a partner, sit together so that you won't get caught bidding against each other. Husbands and wives, sitting apart with friends, may unknowingly bid each other up to double what they would have paid had one known that the other was bidding. The game is three-sided at best, so don't make it a four-sided proposition. There is enough to contend with between the auctioneer, yourself, and your opposition. If you sit toward the rear you can see where the opposition bidders are sitting, or what part is against you. If you spot someone as a dealer, you can almost always feel safe in going beyond his bid. He will be practical and will not often bid beyond 60 to 70 per cent of what he will have to sell the article for in his shop. If in your shopping you have found that an oldtime hutch cabinet sells for about $300, plan to make $200 your limit; when the bidding gets to about $150, wait to see what happens. If there are still several anxious bidders, hold off and wait for another day unless bidding stops below your figure. On the other hand, by careful timing you may not waken the opposition and possibly the piece will go for as little as $100. It is all a gamble and the bidding might be, for all anyone knows, controlled by the astrological makeup of the stars.

Break down the auction into four component parts:

1. The Auctioneer who runs the show. He is wise and probably expert. His fame and fortune depend upon how much money he can extract from the wares auctioned. At the beginning of the auction he will probably put the crowd through a little workout to feel the pulse of the day. He knows most true values and he will try to find out how much

ANOTHER ANTIQUE WILL BE BORN BY 1980!

I think so anyway. It is graceful and has good lines. And it is now useful and in excellent condition. Not an original, it was made about 1880. Few of its brothers and sisters are left.

No longer does this lady's small writing desk hide its light under a bushel; it has been stripped, repaired, and refinished. When found, its finish was badly checked and almost blackened. No one would have known that it was attractive solid mahogany with a matching veneered top. Minor repairs were made to the pigeonhole affair inside. It was stripped with my recommended water-washing method, and allowed to dry, and then lightly stained with a brown color-in-oil and a "pinch" of blue to give it a slight honey hue. As you read on, you will learn how easy it is to make almost any hue with color-in-oil and paint thinner.

The small solid mahogany chair that goes with this desk is seen in a sequence of photographs on pages 140–143 that give you an idea of the ease of stripping when the proper paint remover and method are used, the way to stain good wood better, and the way to seal the stain and then to apply the first finish coating. In short, from stripping to final finish in one day!

the crowd knows before he offers the better items. He will probably first offer some "doo-dabs" in an attempt to expose the audience's temper and knowledge. Study his timing, his stance, and his pitch. He wants your dollars badly—all of them—but at the same time he won't let you down. He will probably entertain you along the way, too.

2. The Attending Dealers. They will always be found at any important country auction and most city or town auctions, as well. They will make sharp, snappy bids usually, and you can sometimes recognize them from the attitude of the auctioneer who probably knows them or can spot a dealer from his own experience. Others in the audience can also indicate them to you. In any case, before a half hour has elapsed you can probably sense who the dealers are. They have to be practical, and if you know market values you will find that they do not exceed 70 per cent of what the average value is.

3. The Gamblers. As at horse races, there are a few who find auctions their gambling outlet. They like to "play" the auctions every day, and play they do. Regardless of value, they will continue to bid until they have won. If you attempt to compete with them, you will find yourself in a dollar donnybrook. Whatever the gamblers win by bidding, it will probably be carried to some local dealer and sold for half what they paid for it. You will always be the loser if you compete with these automatic bidders.

4. The Show. That is exactly what an auction can be to some people. They attend auctions for the show, or maybe they have no other way of being with people and seeing any action. They never make a bid but just sit and watch. They must get some sort of fun from it, or possibly it is just a relief from TV. Don't let them confuse you.

After you have attended several auctions you will understand more than these oversimplified assessments. You will find fun and delight in the details as you grow more observant and become a connoisseur of auctioneers. You will learn to pick your way as you go over the stock to be auctioned. Sometimes you can be more alert than the auctioneer, and certainly you can be sharper than the average auction-goer. On an inspection tour I once noted a nice small Oriental rug rolled the wrong way so that two uncut threads looked like a major defect. I must have been the only one to unroll the rug to look at it and make sure that there were no defects. The auctioneer, in the heat of the job, did not notice the situation and when it was put up for bid, the "defects" were there for all to see. I had decided the true value was probably $35 and opened the bid with $3. Everyone else was looking at the "defects" and no one bid, although the auctioneer did his best to make them up the first bid. I was stuck with a good bargain—although I had the grace to be a little sheepish about it. Such are the ways of auctions.

3. *FURNITURE CONSTRUCTION*

A "joiner" is a person who makes woodwork and furniture, particularly a skilled workman. "Joinery" is the term for such work. There are many ways in which the various pieces that compose furniture can be put together; some are good, some are faulty. The way in which furniture is joined can also indicate the probable age of the piece. The charts or sketches in this section will give you a graphic idea of what kinds of joints are strong or weak, which are good and which are bad ways of joining wood to form pieces of furniture.

For storage pieces, drawers must be formed in boxlike structures whose durability and usefulness will depend largely upon how the sides and bottoms are constructed. The upright sides of the boxes can be held in various ways, but certain ones are better than others. Similarly there are various points to look for in construction of the frames of desks and bureaus, in joining rungs, spokes, splats, rails, and arms. As with every set of rules, there are exceptions which must be made in what to look for in joinery. American country furniture is often quite crudely put together; the very crudity and primitive joining of the corners and others parts can prove quite positively its authenticity and classic construction. The more refined, or parlor-style pieces may be indicative of certain other styles. In Early American country furniture the corners of drawers or other boxlike forms may simply consist of two pieces of wood placed at right angles with long hand-wrought iron nails, carefully centered on the opposing piece, holding them together. In general, one-inch-thick clear pine boards were used, although other local woods might have been employed occasionally. Although this method is not any great feat of engineering, such construction is authentic and usually adds to the value of the piece of furniture. The boards may be quite rough and even warped. Do not pass up hutches, jelly cabinets, blanket chests, or dry sinks with joinery of this sort if you value Early American furniture.

The following definitions will help to identify, with the aid of the sketches, what is meant by the various terms which designate the kinds of joinery used in furniture.

PRIMITIVE or very early Colonial. Two thick boards put together, held flush by hand-wrought iron nails. Not high-class cabinet work but of value in Early American or country-style furniture.

RABBET (or rebate) corner construction employs a grove, or slot, cut in the end of one board to receive the end of another board. Nails as well as glue may be used to hold such corners together. Not a sound method but often used in cheap, poorly constructed furniture. It is often the cause of drawers sticking.

DOVETAILING is the best corner invented to date. Modern machine tools make perfectly fitting dovetails that are slightly roundish. The oldtime dovetailing done by hand is more irregular, sometimes noticeably so. It is easy to see why such a joint is strong, durable, and holds the corner at right angles. Glue is used to insure tightness and durability.

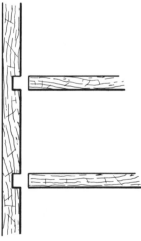

HOUSING is the term used for a slot cut in the sides and fronts of drawers, often on the back piece as well, in which the bottom board is fitted.

SLOTTED JOINT is the term for a slot cut into the upright sides of bookshelves to admit the shelf board. If not well done, shelves may be weak and wobbly.

TONGUE-AND-GROOVE FITTING may be familiar because it is the way modern floor boards are fitted together. Paneling on furniture is often fitted together in this manner. The thin panel in this case would form the "tongue" which fits into the "groove" or slot cut into the framing members.

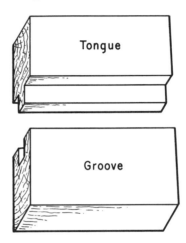

MORTISE-AND-TENON JOINT (sometimes spelled "mortice") is excellent for joining two heavy pieces. Used for stretchers of large pieces of furniture and at times found in old hand-crafted pieces with the tenon extending completely through the hole, or mortise, of the supporting member.

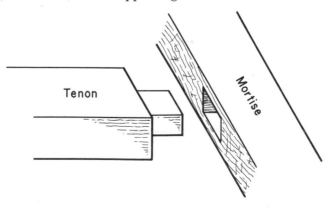

DOWELING is also a method of jointing. Similar to mortise-and-tenon, in that a peg is inserted into a round hole bored in the other member, large or small pegs, or dowels, are used and often more than one may be employed. Snugly fitted and glued into their holes, they figure in much old construction, giving furniture strength. Often a mortise-and-tenon joint is also doweled from the sides, as in the sketch below, to insure strength and to keep the tenon from withdrawing from the mortise when under strain.

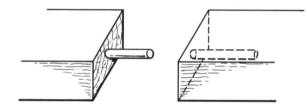

RABBETING for flange work for fitting boards together is also strong and durable if the slotting is wide enough and if doweling is added from the sides, where this is desirable. Too often such flange rabbeting is poorly done, too narrow, and glue depended on for holding it together.

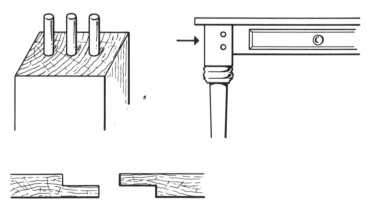

What Are Good Cabinetmakers' Woods?

As a good seamstress must know the great differences in textiles—wools, silks, cottons, and synthetics—and their capacities; as a good mechanic knows the differences and similarities of engines and their quirks; so must a good refinisher have some working knowledge of the woods commonly used in furniture. Such primary knowledge will be important to you and will save your time and money.

It is not necessary that a refinisher should become an expert in identifying the various kinds of woods, unless he chooses to for his own personal satisfaction and enjoyment, but some differences should be recognized, such as graining, porosity, flexibility, strength, and texture. Without this elementary knowledge the final results of refinishing may leave much to be desired. There are excellent books on woods, some of them with lifelike reproductions of woods to make identification easier, and these may be consulted by those who wish to pursue the subject. The main reason for learning about woods is that the modern refinisher must know about the reactions of the recommended chemicals on the woods so that the hours of labor will be well repaid.

Many species of trees have been cut and made into lumber for use in making furniture, ranging from bamboo, balsa, butternut, and basswood to teak, tulip, and tamarack. However, because we are concerned here with only the most useful elements of this vast subject, I have compiled a list of the woods most commonly used in making good American furniture:

Birch	Mahogany	Rosewood
Cherry	Maple	Walnut
Chestnut	Oak	Whitewood
Hickory	Pine	

Of these eleven woods only six are of great importance—cherry, mahogany, maple, oak, pine, and walnut. These are the woods you will encounter most frequently in refinishing, repairing, and stripping furniture. From a practical point of view, there are actually only two comparisons to make: Is the wood hard or soft? Is it porous or nonporous? To qualify these questions, let us admit immediately that all woods are porous to a degree or they could not be finished. Also, all woods are hard to a degree, as we all remember from the days when father used his paddle. Furniture must have wood which is hard or it would never stand up under use and abuse. But the usual classification of hardwood and softwood is our goal here.

Five of the six woods above are classified as hardwoods, pine being the exception. Pine, a softwood, will need extra attention prior to staining and this is detailed under the section on Staining. (See pages 106 and 167.) As to porosity, only two woods need give us much trouble—oak and mahogany which have large open pores. Walnut pores are smaller but more open than some other woods. This means that they will need a wood filler to bring them up to the surface level before putting on the surface coats. After the filler has dried and is hard, the entire surface can be smoothed.

Sometimes the wood gives an excellent clue to the antiquity of the piece and consequently may be vital in determining its value. From the early 1600s to the middle 1700s walnut was the commonly used wood but about the middle of the eighteenth century, from, say, 1750 onward, mahogany replaced it in favor. These were, of course, woods for the parlor furniture, not the everyday or country furniture. Later on the wood most favored was rosewood, expensive and with an interesting grain. If you can find an old rosewood piano, it will be high priced, and in early Victorian furniture a great deal of rosewood was used for parlor furniture—whatnots, bookshelves, and other pieces.

Chestnut is also a good wood and a great deal of it was used in place of walnut, where that was not available or chestnut was cheaper locally. It was a sad day in the late nineteenth century when the native chestnuts began to succumb to a fungus disease and so many of them were killed. Gumwood, beechwood, and fruit woods were all used locally and in the latter part of the nineteenth century much whitewood was used for furniture. Whitewood is a broad classification, taking in many different species of trees, all softwood. Much of the whitewood in the United States comes from the South and is probably one of two woods, that from the tulip tree or that from the linden or basswood. These trees grow quickly and are sturdy, often being used for frames or where they can be covered with veneers of more valuable woods. Much of the better grades can be stained to imitate the hardwoods with which they are teamed.

In staining woods, here are some suggestions that may guide you in coloring the woods in a manner most suited to their natures. If you have an antique piece that is being refinished, try to observe and match the color of the woods before all the finish is removed so that you can keep its original character.

Walnut is best in brown shades, light or dark, according to choice.

Mahogany may be dark brown or dark reddish-brown.

Maple is most authentic in the dark honey shades, but may be seen as well in slightly reddish tones, pale honey, or in yellowish tones.

Pine may be kept to almost its natural pale tone or stained in light brown or tan tones.

Cherry is favored in bright reddish tones, although sometimes in yellow or brown.

Whitewood is stained to match the veneers and other woods or, if used alone, can be in the modern fruit-wood browns and tans.

In your searches for antiques you may run across the term "married piece." When this is applied to furniture, it means that only part of the piece is original, although the "spouse" may be antique, too. For instance, it is most frequently applied to chairs. The original may have been made with one or two woods, but the foundation was broken. Another chair of a similar style or of the same period, perhaps with whole legs but a broken back, might have been available, so the legs of this chair were salvaged and stuck onto the chair with the whole seat and back. Perhaps the opposite might have been the case, or in extreme cases, the seat might be from one chair, the back from another, and the legs from a third, though this is not often encountered. The legs used might have been shorter, fatter, or somewhat out of character, but they would have done if they were of a good wood and if they were well made. Not all of these graftings might have taken place recently—some may be of long standing—and not all of them might have been done to preserve values by using old woods and antique parts for value's sake alone; many might be the result of expediency. The old craftsmen were men of action with little time or inclination to build vocabularies but their few quoted utterances always seem to hit the nail on the head. One old chair-maker expressed a great deal in his simple words: "Good wood stood."

PART *II*

Refinishing Techniques

4. WHY REFINISH FURNITURE?

I gambled that someone would ask this question, so I have prepared an answer. My task has been light, compared with that of convincing someone that he should like golf, fishing, knitting, sewing, camping, sailing, skiing, gardening, or painting: you must be interested in refinishing furniture or you would not have picked up this book. Each person should have his own choice of action, but I am certain that all who join our ranks will find the following propositions logical, and any lingering doubts will be dissolved along with the first coat of paint removed from an antique piece of furniture.

Refinishing is an extracurricular activity that can be followed with complete relaxation and enjoyment whenever one finds time for it. Sound economics are built into the hobby and it is a full outlet for personal conquest and accomplishment. It might be an unconscious drive to reintroduce our hands to our mind, but it is mainly a gentle diversion whose goal is self-expression. Whether refinishing furniture may be defined as an art, a craft, or a science is impossible to tell; it is beside the point, anyhow. Whatever the name by which it may be called, it is good for the heart, the ego, the hand, and the pocketbook. It is a tonic for mind and body as well as a constructive hobby.

If any further demonstration is needed, you might look at Sir Winston Churchill's hobbies. How about his painting? And how about his hobby of laying bricks? Even as he dealt with the superhuman problems of war and of government he occasionally took time off to paint some pictures and to do some bricklaying. He knew his therapeutics as well as he understood war, words, politics, and people, and his vigor of mind and body lasted for ninety years. Churchill was a free man because he kept himself that way, and you can be the same. Just remember that if such accomplishment can be attained by working with the cool smoothness of mortar and bricks, what results can you achieve by renewing a shapely piece of mahogany, pine, or walnut in your own workshop? Even if you have no workshop, you can still refinish antiques. Plenty of people who live in city apartments do it all the time—it just requires a little more patience and care.

Our ancestors were plain-spoken men. Their viewpoint, expressed in nearly as many words, was: "If you want something done well, do it yourself, dammit." In today's labor market, with slapdash workmen willing to take our money but not to do an honest job, it becomes more necessary than ever to do our own work. We become more like our ancestors all the time. The early American farmer in the wilderness had to be his own doctor, veterinarian, tinsmith, blacksmith, locksmith, machinist, toolmaker, shoemaker, butcher, botanist, weatherman, hunter, designer, architect, plumber, chemist, and food producer—in addition to being his own cabinetmaker and furniture finisher.

Refinishing can save money, too. Consider a chair, a well-crafted one, if you can find a good one today. Wouldn't you expect to pay at least $60 for it if you purchased it brand new? Would you buy one in an antique shop or at auction for $30 or less? If you went to the right auction you might possibly bring one home for $10. With a few additional dollars and a little patient effort you can put it into first-class condition. Similar savings can result from buying antiques or reproductions and refinishing them—sofas, stands, tables, bureaus, and bric-a-brac of many kinds. There are few other ways to save a sizable amount of money so creatively or so constructively. And if you keep track of the money saved and invest it or put it in the bank, you will be getting dividends in money as well as in the improvement in your health and mental outlook.

This book puts forth some entirely new rules for the refinisher so that he can have the best possible collection of furniture costing the least in time, labor, and money. It may raise some eyebrows here and there, and I hope it will raise the sights of the general public so that they will demand better refinishing products and profit by the ease and the safety they can thus obtain. Exchanging the cumbersome rules and procedures of the past for the new chemical methods will break some old rules, such as, "You can't mix water with oil." Right in our home laundries we mix oil and water every day, so why not put the idea to work elsewhere? It has now been thoroughly tested.

Refinishing is a major part of the restoration of antiques and good refinishing frequently requires the entire removal of old finishes. The old bugaboo is now put to flight—paint removal and stripping need no longer be a gooey, toxic, or discouraging mess. Because of so many misconceptions and the lack of clear directions in the past, many people have understandably shied away from furniture with defective surfaces. But the application of wood stains, and the proper application of new finishes, are no more difficult today than most of the other things we do routinely. If you can wield an ordinary paint brush and use steel wool and a bucket of suds, then there is fun and excitement and a true reward in refinishing furniture. The refinishing and restoration of antiques no longer require antique methods!

What Is Worth Refinishing?

Most antiques are worth the time, the effort, and the expense of refinishing. What are the exceptions? This question can best be answered by your own capacities, your desires, and your needs. Will the finished piece serve a vital and important function in your home? Obviously it will be worthwhile if it can serve you in this way. Are you careful and able to use your hands well enough to achieve good results? Then go ahead with assurance. Is it worth the expense, as well as the effort? Here there is a common-sense rule that may help. As the ratio between intrinsic value and original cost rises in favor of value, more and more reparable damage can be accepted in the piece. In other words, if the article might be worth $100 after reclamation and the cost of obtaining it was perhaps $50, we might consider a normal amount of repair. If, on the other hand, the article might be worth in the neighborhood of $500 after repair, then considerable expense and effort might be put forth to repair and refinish the piece. The key word here, of course, is "reparable" damage.

Work and effort must balance in considering refinishing from a standpoint of economics. Shy away from badly broken, poorly constructed, rotten, cumbersome pieces that may require strange or unusual repairs. Accept anything at a bargain price that has a friendly face, dirty or not, and try to put it back to work again. Naturally one would prefer to get a fine Colonial with a sound heart, but it would not be common sense to turn down anything of Early American or truly country style, or a sound Victorian piece, if the price were low and if no irreparable features could be detected upon examination. Even a reproduction made in the 1920s that survived the 1929 stock market crash without so much as a broken arch would be acceptable, if it had good lines and fulfilled the need of the household. Be utilitarian and sharpen your judgment. If a chair has graceful lines and needs only a bit of tightening at the joints, or possibly refinishing, it is a good buy. A sudsy bath of detergent followed by a rubdown with a turpentine-and-linseed-oil-soaked cloth may be all that will be needed. But if the wood has been saturated with oil or grease, if it has deep scratches, mars, wide cracks, or noticeable warping, hesitate a bit longer unless it is a giveaway piece. It might not repay the effort of refinishing. If there has been cheap construction—rabbeted drawer corners, bottoms not housed—or if the wood seems "dead," perhaps from caustic baths of potash or lye, or from being tortured by rain, sleet, or snow in some backyard, step aside. If the former owner did not respect it, it may be beyond redemption now. If the construction employed too many nails or screws, or if the wood is brittle from living next to an overheated steam radiator—cherry wood is especially susceptible—then it is wiser to gamble on something better coming up at the next auction or being found on the next antiquing expedition.

Look instead for good dovetailing, doweling, mortise-and-tenon joints as well as for the shapely outlines and the antiquity, the decoration, and design. Accept a few holes, what might be called an "undernourished skin condition," a bit of wobbling and squeaks, a few light scratches and mars; if the price is right, it is probably still a good buy. For the more adept worker, a piece can safely be brought back into condition even if it is no longer sure-footed, if it is not actually down on bended knee, so to speak. Common-sense chemistry, some sanding papers, and the glue bottle will turn the trick. Even if a rung of a chair is missing, for a modest fee you can probably find someone to turn a new one that will match, if you cannot do it yourself.

To sum up some common-sense rules to remember when making a purchase of antique or old furniture:

1. Avoid furniture held together at corners and joints by modern nails and screws. (The exception is primitive furniture, where this is a part of the style and construction of the

furniture.) Avoid furniture with rabbeted corners, and look for dovetailing. Look for tongue-and-groove joining of boards, and panels with such construction; look for mortise-and-tenon joints, and for doweling and dowel joints which make jointure secure.

2. With upholstered furniture, allow practically no value if the frame is wobbly or unsound, even if the springs are silent.

3. Inspect veneer (thin sheets of quality wood glued over cheaper and rougher woods) and if it is badly cracked or warped, it will require expert work to renew it. If the veneer is found on a nineteenth-century piece, then it was probably laid on with water glues and should be easily removed for restoration. If the piece is only fifty to seventy-five years old, then it is likely that waterproof glues were used and the veneer will be difficult to remove. In that case, however, the veneer is not likely to be subject to much warping and splitting—one of man's few modern improvements in furniture. If some parts of the veneer are missing, as on the edge of a table, a projecting part of a dresser, or the frame of an antique sofa, the veneer can be matched and replaced. See the list of suppliers (page 206) for sources of such supplies.

4. If an old piece is saturated with oil or grease, the wood swollen or stained beyond probable restoration, or if the wood is a dead gray or greenish color (from a caustic bath?), do not buy it.

5. Rough oak is hard to finish. Sometimes it is badly cut, probably against the grain. This means you can never get it down to a smooth, fine finish. It might be good enough for a paint job, but buying a ream of sanding paper is expensive, and that quantity would be required for producing a clear, smooth finish.

6. Cherry wood, despite its obvious beauty, is a problem. It is very subject to a complete drying out, with a conse-

quent loss of strength. It will crack and crack forever, when it is brittle; the wood "died" from being subjected to a hostile environment—probably it was kept too near a hot radiator or other source of heat.

7. Select furniture for its firmness, good shape, and flexibility as well as to satisfy your taste. Easterners are generally avid collectors of Colonial designs, and the early country styles such as Shaker; often they do not favor Empire or Mission. Texans swoon over Empire; Californians and other westerners like Mission style; and there must be a mass of modern buyers who like Grand Rapids, for it is now in antique shops across the land. Whatever your choice, keep in mind that the wood should be sound and the damages reparable.

8. Check the pieces thoroughly to assess their strength and also to check their antiquity. For real antiquity, the wider and rougher the dovetailing, the older it may be. Inspect the bottoms and sides of drawers; in general, the darker the natural wood, the older it is. Check the backs of bureaus, chests, desks, and cabinets or hutches for saw marks on the wood as a sign of antiquity. Backs were seldom finished because of the work involved and because pieces were set against the walls. If the saw marks visible on the wood are curved, then you may be sure the piece was made less than a hundred years ago. If they are straight, then you probably have a real antique with the wood sawed up and down by hand. The darkness of the wood is sometimes called "patina," darkening from the atmosphere only. If the woods inside the piece are bright and new-looking, then the piece is not old—though it may be just the bargain you are looking for if the lines are right and construction is honest.

9. If the piece has old, worn stenciling, do not take it off. If it is a really old piece, you will be removing part of its value. If not, then perhaps you will want to try to copy or

simulate what is there. Suggestions for stenciling appear in Chapter 16.

10. If the piece is covered with the original coat of paint, this may also be an asset. The oldtime makers often painted their furniture with their own red, green, or black paint, particularly a very sound chair that had a pine seat, birch legs, and an ash back, in order to give it smoothness and a uniform appearance. If such old paints are firm or not worn or scratched too badly, do not remove them because you have a true sign of antiquity that adds to the value of the piece. The paint would probably indicate that the furniture was made in the late 1700s or early 1800s. Just wash the piece carefully and give it a coat of paste wax from time to time to preserve the paint. There is a section on old paints in Appendix IV, to let you know what kind was used.

Rather than try to cover every possible facet of this interesting subject, I suggest that you consult as many books as you can or listen to all the knowledgeable antique dealers you may encounter in your shopping expeditions. Ask questions about joining, gain experience in identifying dovetailing, doweling, tongue-and-groove, mortise-and-tenon and the other kinds of joints used in old pieces. It will add to your pleasure as you become expert, and certainly add to the expertness with which you choose the antiques you want to own and refinish.

5. PATINA—A TRAP
FOR REFINISHERS

The word "patina," like the word "antique," may have many interpretations and definitions. Probably the most acceptable definition of "antique" is something old—from almost anywhere in the past—and, presumably, something desirable and useful. But we perceive even less what is in some people's minds when they employ the word "patina." It is not so much that it is an inexact word, as that interpretations vary so widely in its use. Perhaps we can give it a certain focus.

Where did this strange word come from? Well, it did not originate in the furniture or antique furniture field because it has had a well-defined meaning in the metal trades for centuries. There it denotes a film or incrustation on bronze or copper, usually greenish, and in the trade it has also come to mean a perfection of the sheen or finish given to the surface of a metal object. No one knows for sure when this word was borrowed by the antique sellers and cabinet-makers, but it must be comparatively recent—say within the last seventy years or so. Modern dictionaries now list a secondary definition for "patina": a film or coloring produced in the course of time on wood or other substances. There is even a third accepted usage for the word: it can also mean a surface appearance caused by aging or mellowing and in this meaning it can be used for everything from wood to marble, and even rugs. Since "patina" is a term bandied about frequently, it is wise not to enter antiquing circles in ignorance of it, especially after reading this book.

First of all the pronunciation: you will hear "pateena," "patinna," "pateen," and "patyna." Take your choice—it will probably mean you are using a French, an Italian, an English, or an American pronunciation. In the antique world, all it means is how a piece of wood looks to you— young, middle-aged, or old. If you can detect a mellower glow to the wood that denotes greater age, as some people claim they can, then you can also detect a nice patina from a bad one—and probably see through the finish that is on the wood. If you take the meaning concerned with darkening of woods, it is a fact that woods darken in varying degrees with age, particularly if they have been filled through the years with all the oils and greases of use—hair oils, cosmetic oils, salad and other eating oils, as well as the dirt that accumulates in the wood pores.

In one book I read, which covers this subject extensively, I learned that it takes about one hundred years for wood to age enough to acquire a nice patina. This caused me to wonder if the author had read about the curator who had set one hundred years as the proper age for an antique. I look at it this way. Take a banana and cut it; it will be creamy white at first, but how does it look after exposure to the elements for four or five hours? Similarly, apples that are cut and exposed will brown to different hues in various lengths of time. And so will woods—pine, maple, mahogany, and all the others.

It seems that everyone has taken up the word patina now, even the manufacturers of the cheaper scrape-off removers. They advise against using water in stripping (which would do no good with their products) for fear of "losing the patina." Believe me, you will not lose your nice patina if you strip with water as suggested in the section on water-washing methods of finish removal (see Chapter 9). All that will be lost will be the old finish in a much easier and quicker way, with less expense and more safely, too. Other experts warn that you must never strip a piece of furniture of its finish and thus eradicate the old patina. They claim it is better to live with the cracks, checking, and terrible old finish forever. Is that the way to treat a nice piece of wood from a good old cabinetmaker's shop? No! And with a little work I think I can prove it.

Look right through the kind of patina that some people sigh over and take pride in. By their expressions, they must be referring to antiques; therefore age is involved. But does that kind of person know where this antique has been all this time? Could the reason for that "soft and mellow patina" have been any of the following: an oil stove, pancake batter, wood ashes, axle grease, coal smoke, or old-fashioned sticky hair pomade? Is patina possibly just 1890 kerosene spilled from a lamp? I would rather take a chance and get a finish that will bring out the true beauty of the wood, such as it had in the beginning. What caused the darkening of the wood inside the drawers? Very probably the piece was kept in a dirty room for years or left to the weather in a leaky shed next to the smoke-curing house.

One author, a furniture repairman for many years, writes that he was caught in the patina trap for over twenty years until one time when he tried to match up old woods to repair an antique chair. The chair was one of a set, and he was forced to insert new woods. After he was finished, "in spite of the fine patina which I thought could not be matched, I could not pick out the damaged chair from the set," he writes.

Going along the road of common sense, we find that one type of pine will darken quicker and different from another species of pine. When we strip this, we will take away that part of the patina caused by grease and dirt, smoke, or oil, but not the coloration and surface caused by age. The surface portions detailed can be duplicated easily, while the latter, caused by age, remain. The insides of drawers and furniture pieces can give one clues to antiquity, but it is a fact that, given the right conditions, one piece of pine only fifty years old can look older than another piece of pine two hundred years old.

I hope I have clarified this mysterious subject a bit. The main thing to remember is that common-sense refinishing will remove all the old dirt, axle grease, hand cream, hair oils, fats, oils, and fumes that are stuck in the varnish or other finish, but that honest patina will be left because age has produced it. It comes from good clean wood and a good clear finish that shows the wood—a combination that cannot be beaten. Let's not be foiled by oil!

6. SHOULD THE FINISH
BE REMOVED?

Stripping off old finishes may not always be necessary, nor in certain cases is it wise. If the old finish is intact, covering the entire surface, that is, not too badly scarred and marred, it can often be used with a minimum of restoration. In the case of original antiques, really old and authenticated as to maker, the original finish is often an asset, for the value might shrink as much as 50 per cent if the finish is removed and replaced. This is particularly true of old pieces with decorated, painted finishes. Here the value may lie almost entirely in the original finish, with only a token or fragment of the value being in the wood, the design of the piece itself, or the age. Therefore caution is indicated in deciding whether or not to take off the old finish. If you think you may have acquired a truly choice piece, one made by a famous maker or something of museum quality, have it authenticated or appraised before you do anything drastic to it. On the other hand, with most antiques which are primarily purchased for use as well as for their beauty and age, putting the finish into good repair or refinishing a piece which has been badly scarred or allowed to weather and lose the protection the wood should have, will bring it back into use and restore its beauty, making it take a new lease on life and preserving it for future generations to use and admire.

If the article is truly old, the chances are good that the original finish (on clear-finished wood, that is) was shellac. If it was a painted piece, the chances are that the colored paint was what is commonly called "milk," "buttermilk," or "refractory" paint. Shellac can be easily taken off with alcohol, since that is its original solvent. The ordinary commercial alcohol which can be bought by the pint, quart, or gallon can at the paint store is what is required. First make a test by rubbing on alcohol with a soft cloth in an inconspicuous spot over a very small area. If the finish softens and starts to come off on the cloth, you can go ahead with the alcohol and remove it. Sop it on with a brush or cloth, and then as the shellac softens, use fine steel wool pads dipped in alcohol to remove the sludge. After most of it is off a washdown and rubdown with cloths dipped in alcohol will do the final job of removal. Alcohol is somewhat toxic, too, so good ventilation should be provided.

With varnishes, lacquers, and painted finishes, often all that is needed is a good washing down to remove all the accumulated gummy dirt from the surface. Unless the surface is badly marred, checked, or alligatored, washing it thoroughly with a mild soap and water will remove all such dirt on the surface. Dry it with soft cloths and then take a look at it. If the finish shows the grain of the wood well and is intact, a polishing or two with a hard paste wax will often be all that is necessary to bring it back into use. Some refinishers rub down varnished or lacquered furniture with a mixture of 50 per cent boiled linseed oil and 50 per cent turpentine for the final coat, just after the soap and water washdown. When this has dried thoroughly, the surface can be waxed. This, too, is worth trying before buying paint remover and stripping. With painted furniture, of course, only the water and soap washing would be used before waxing, not the boiled linseed oil and turpentine rubdown.

Reproductions and other furniture made in the 1920s which have the original finish intact might have been finished with lacquer, which gives a beautiful clear finish when properly applied. If this finish must be removed, use lacquer thinner which will take it off as easily as shellac is removed by alcohol. Thinner is available at paint stores and some hardware shops. Because there is some toxicity in the fumes, again be sure to maintain good ventilation and be sure to wear heavy rubber gloves.

Should your antique piece need to have the finish stripped and you do not have facilities or wish not to be bothered with paint removal—a problem in the small apartment, for instance—there are professional furniture-stripping shops in most cities and often in suburban communities, as well. Most of them are reliable, responsible, and efficient. The fee is not great, merely commensurable with the work to be done.

The professional scene has taken a new spurt of life in recent years with the advent of efficient chemical removers. The breakthrough occurred with the destruction of the old bugaboo about oil not mixing with water. Since the day the new water emulsifiers, called "surfactants," appeared it has become quite evident that various chemicals from oils found in paints and paint removers can easily mix with other substances which can then be carried off by water. This water emulsification process has made stripping so efficient that the amateur refinisher can now remove the sludge, similar to the process used by the up-to-date professional furniture-strippers. The professionals know that these surfactants change the normal surface tension of any drop of water radically, and this is what has altered the method of scraping off sludge, which was once very costly and time consuming, replacing it with the faster and smoother water-washing methods.

Previously the furniture-stripper was located in an out-of-the-way place where he used what was called a "hot-dip" tank which was filled with water and strong, damaging caustics such as potash, lye, metasilicate, or soda ash. These quickly dissolved almost any film of paint or varnish, the furniture being immersed for varying periods of time according to the number of layers of old finish and also the type of finish used. After the immersion, the article was washed down with water to expose the wood, which was probably now a dirty gray or darkened to some degree. Good woods were less good and often the glue was damaged so that unless the piece was taken apart and reglued there would be a looseness and probably a chorus of squeaks in the joints when the piece was used.

These old practices are now no longer necessary and are less and less used. Some of the older shops for stripping now employ the new methods but many of these are also devoted to general repair, improvement, or staining and color-matching finishes. The stripping department is only part of the work they do. The newer stripping shops do only stripping of finishes. Most shops today are not set up on a production-line basis and will follow similar procedures to the ones detailed in this book. They all work for perfection and could never afford or permit the use of a caustic bath. It would be well, however, to inquire about the method to be used before committing a piece to a professional. The type of paint remover he uses may be slightly different from those recommended here, but they will probably be similar. He may use a pumping process and more solvent, rather than the hand-brushing method; and he will use hand scraping only for the old, fragile, water-glued veneers.

I have in my own workshop used something of the methods employed by professionals. I assembled an assortment of furniture with many different kinds of finishes, all needing refinishing. I was able to strip them in about 20 per cent of the time it would have taken to do them singly. The total was nineteen chairs, a large hutch, a dining-table top, a settee, and a three-drawer dresser. But even though I have a modest but well-equipped home shop, I admit that a wise professional can do the work faster. That is why I say that if you cannot do your stripping at home, investigate the possibilities of having a professional stripping job. But do not give up the entire satisfaction of finishing—you can still apply the final finish and enjoy that accomplishment as well as save money. And you may find, with a little ingenuity and care, that you can strip the antique, too.

7. ABOUT OLD FINISHES AND PAINT REMOVERS

In every one of man's endeavors there are one or two major and critical maneuvering points that will turn the tide in his favor, if he will only recognize them. It is true, is it not, that almost any able-bodied person can play golf, fish, ski, or sail a boat? Why, then, does one golfer play with grace and ease, averaging a score of 74, while another, who has put just as much energy into the game, will have such a struggle to keep his score under 100, perspiring all the way? There are many factors, of course, but part of the answer lies in the fact that the one who wins consistently is the one who wraps the wisest and best-trained hands around a golf club. It is equally true that the person who wants to have success with refinishing antiques—and anyone can play at this game, too—will do well to inform himself beforehand. The one who knows the most about the nature and eccentricities of finishes and paint removers is automatically paving his way toward more enjoyment, less work, and much better final results. In over thirty years of experience with refinishing, I have noted an increasing trend toward avoiding the most important step in restoration: the stripping of paint or other finish from the wood. Why is this?

Maybe too many people have been misled through misinformation or lack of information into thinking that stripping paint is a dirty, difficult, complicated undertaking. Such should not be the case. But stripping will always be rough and tough work until people know first of all what

54

they are attempting to remove and, second, what chemical stripping material is best to use. Any golfer quickly learns not to use a putter for his drives or a bulky wood for his putting.

Stripping can be easy once the shroud of mystery is lifted from the old paint and varnish finishes and commercial paint removers assessed for their usefulness and various qualities. The pages which follow will attempt to clarify both subjects. Even though the messages may be long, they will shorten your labors because you will have a full understanding of what you are trying to accomplish. In this assessment, you will not find value in any of the usual statements for paint removers, such as, "Use any paint remover," "Apply a commercial paint remover," "No afterwash necessary," "Get the safe one," "It is easier on the hands," "Use semi-paste," or "Just apply paint remover." The history of this craft is littered with statements similar to those, so that even "experts" are still working in the dark sometimes. One "authority" wrote in his book, "The astonishing thing is that the paint remover has no ill effects on the skin. You don't have to worry about it getting on your hands or your clothes." The liquid remover was referred to by brand name, and it was—and still is—a highly toxic and flammable substance. There was no indication that anything toxic could be absorbed through the skin, inhaled, or otherwise introduced into the body to cause sickness, irreparable harm, or possibly even death if such a remover were used carelessly. We find "astonishing" a very mild word in this instance.

Another "expert," teaching refinishing on a television program, recommended to the public a certain paint remover because it was a semi-paste type, without wax. (Wax is an enemy to good refinishing.) I happen to know for a fact that the brand of paint remover that he recommended is loaded with more wax than most paint removers. Even the teacher had been fooled and confused, probably because the manufacturer did not specify "wax" on his product but used a little-known coined word in place of it. The manufacturer is using 100 per cent wax and the television audience is bound once again to experience failure in refinishing.

There are many instances of irresponsibility in statements found on packages of paint removers. One well-known kind states: "Removes all paint from all objects." It may remove some shellacs, some lacquers, and varnishes, but it is absolutely impossible for this particular remover to remove paint from all objects. It would be interesting to see the manufacturer demonstrate his remover on a piece of antique furniture with some of the old milk paints on it. If a toothpick manufacturer was so energetic in his sales as to state that his product was strong enough to lift the Rock of Gibraltar, would he be believed? There is not much exaggeration between this comparison and some of the statements I have seen. Another paint remover states: "Use with absolute safety anywhere." The Food and Drug Administration of the United States would have some work ahead trying that one out.

If you understand better what kind of finishes you are likely to encounter, you will be able to select the proper paint remover and your score will be improved considerably. Varnishes, lacquers, and shellacs are a class of finish considerably different from thicker paints. In addition, there is a great difference between the removal characteristics of thin layers of modern oil paints and those of the older oilless paints. Read about paints and finishes and arm yourself with knowledge. See Appendix IV.

8. PAINT REMOVERS

        The proper removal of old finishes is often the keystone to good restoration. Therefore it is wise to learn as much as you can about the chemical mixes commonly called "paint removers." How can you restore or refinish with satisfaction over an old, defective finish? The critical step may be the removal of the paint or other finish and now is the time to consider the eventual mess, or the dangers to your health, or both. The common liquid-solvent paint removers found in paint or hardware shops will break the bond of many old finishes by a process of softening, swelling, or actual chemical liquefication, but all of the removing must be done by you. The resulting softening of the paint, commonly called "sludge," is the mess referred to that has so frequently discouraged paint removal novices in the past. It can, however, be efficiently taken care of with comparative ease if some common-sense rules are remembered and applied. Furthermore, as there has been so little said and so frequently so little apparent concern given to the characteristics of the liquid-solvent types of paint removers, I shall attempt enlightenment as to the presence of toxicity to humans and the dangers of flash fires when products of this nature are used.

In most of the articles and books on refinishing which have been published in the past years, the paint remover section was given the least attention, or the subject was very quickly passed over. In my estimation, few users—amateur or professional—really comprehend the full potency of chemical paint removers. The lack of cautions to the users may be likened to telling amateur carpenters to use an electric circular handsaw if many long lengths need to be cut without cautioning about the potential dangers to hands and fingers of this lethal (when improperly used) machine. Let us therefore fully explore paint removers so as to be sure they work for us and not against us. Some writers on the subject advise that *all* paint removers of the liquid-solvent type are good; others merely advise the use of "commercial paint removers"; still others will mention a favorite brand name. Yet there may be vast differences between the various brands of the products which are recommended. More space is given to "saving the patina" or "sandpapering with the wood grain" than to this very vital and basic subject.

On the market today there are many brands of liquid-solvent paint removers, and there are about as many formula variations. Some dealers stock one or two, others may stock a wide array. How can you know which to select? How can you know which will remove the finish most easily, with the least mess and the greatest measure of success while still safeguarding your health and property? After all, you want to finish a piece of furniture, not yourself!

It is my firm belief that many solvent-type paint removers are much too dangerous to recommend for general use in the home workshop. During the many years of my experience I have formed strong opinions, necessarily, on the types and kinds offered and there are some which I would not tolerate in my own workshop under any circumstances. Some mixes even today are much like paint removers advertised early in this century, with the same flash-fire flammability and the high toxicity to humans still incorporated. Below are some of the things to watch out for. First is a charmingly named enemy of mankind's health, a pleasant smelling but deadly toxic and almost explosive solvent called "benzol."

BENZOL. A component in various brands of modern paint removers, although the makers must know about the stealthy perils and the bad qualities inherent in it. Benzol is low in cost in comparison with most of the other common solvents that make up paint remover mixtures. The profit motive might be one factor in its use, but benzol is not only an excellent destroyer of varnish, lacquer, shellac—but also of human life. Therefore, *beware*. Benzol-type paint removers have been in use for many years. Research has shown it to be not only highly flammable, with but a single spark needed to start the fireworks, but also it has been shown that frequent use can produce an accumulative poison in the bloodstream, causing incurable anemia. Benzol can be absorbed through the skin tissue as well as inhaled to enter the body through the lungs. Most packages state that it is best to use benzol in a well-ventilated place, outdoors, and caution against allowing it to stay on the skin, but this is not warning enough. If potential danger is there to any high degree, why use it?

Flammable mixtures should also not be used in the home workshop because a quantity of the mixture will be exposed over a considerable area for some time and the fire potential is therefore greater than merely using a small quantity on a wiping rag. With furnaces and motors operating near the workshop, the danger is increased, for the fumes of such flammable removers can drift down and build up along the baseboards. Professional paint-strippers who use flammable mixtures are generally better set up with ventilators and are careful to keep heaters and spark-generating equipment out of the vicinity.

Read Labels Carefully

Producers of consumer goods have a well-established belief that the average user fails to read, let alone study, the labels on the goods. Even though required by law to state formulas and cautions, most manufacturers feel confident that their sales will remain constant, regardless of the dangers within the package, law or no law. A good rule to follow is this: If you find the paint remover can marked "Highly Flammable," think in terms of a possible explosion or an uncontrollable flash fire. If it says "Flammable," be prepared for a fire that is difficult to control. If you find benzol listed as an ingredient, think in terms of poison, and a high degree of danger. You must be your own guide.

Fortunately, a new set of regulations have recently been put out by the United States Food and Drug Administration under the Federal Hazardous Substances Labeling Act. Individuals can obtain worthwhile knowledge and considerable protection if they will take the trouble to inform themselves and read labels. On liquid-solvent-type paint remover cans, look for the word "Caution" and a brief explanatory sentence. Some cans carry a small symbol of skull and crossbones, along with warnings such as "Poison," "Fatal," "Danger," "Cannot be made nonpoisonous," "Use with adequate ventilation," or some other cautionary phrase. Fire danger is rated in descending ratio: "Highly Flammable," "Flammable," "Combustible," "Nonflammable." Be governed accordingly, for the words have real meaning under the law. No two manufacturers of liquid paint removers will accidentally strike the same formula, exactly. Nevertheless, most of them fall within the same broad category of ingredients. Look at the ingredients listed on the can, mandatory by law, and you will find that they are chiefly acetone, alcohol, benzol, methylene chloride, and toluol. Probably no paint remover can be classified as "completely safe," for what is completely safe? The recommended type of liquid paint remover, however, should be no more dangerous than many other popular and commonly used household products. If it is used properly and wisely, there should not be any fear of harm resulting; also, you will get the maximum paint-stripping results.

A third common-sense rule: Do not be misled by catch phrases such as "Does not raise the grain of the wood," "Does not contain acids," "Cuts deeper," "Cuts faster," "Stays wet longer," or "Semi-paste or cream-type."

Do any of these phrases have any real meaning? Are they important to you? I know of very few, if any, of the so-called "volatile solvents" that would raise the grain of wood; none of their ingredients have this power. None of them have acids, in general, so we are safe on this score, too. What is meant by "cuts deeper" or, as it sometimes is expressed, "cuts in depth"? In testing them on articles with twelve or more layers of paint I found that they did not "cut" as deep as one sixtieth of an inch at a time. Since most finishes are more nearly the thickness of this page of paper, that is not meaningful.

"Cuts faster" has a certain use, but its meaning is of doubtful practicality. If you measure with a stopwatch in seconds as you compare a watery, less expensive remover with a heavy-bodied quality remover, you will find that it does wrinkle up the top layer more quickly. But the top layer is as far as it will penetrate and thus the speed is no sign of efficiency. Do not be fooled by the watch's second hand. If one remover penetrates to the wood in eleven minutes and another takes twelve minutes, how much have you gained? You might save that little minute and then spend hours removing the sludge. The real point at issue is whether or not the remover will *sink all the way to the wood* and also present you with an easily-washed-away sludge, not one that requires hand scraping and reapplication.

"Stays wet longer" is another catch phrase. It is true that some removers do not dry up completely as fast as others, but the wetter one most likely has more wax loading it, and sometimes this can be a disadvantage. "Semi-paste or cream-type," recommended for years, have certain virtues. They are less likely to run than are the watery liquid removers, therefore you have a better chance to apply a thick and even coating of remover. The "paste" part is also likely to be heavily loaded with wax so look for a "heavy-bodied" remover that uses methyl cellulose rather than wax for a thickener. If you wish to, you can quickly find out. Chill the remover to about 40 degrees F. If it is pasty and does not flow without being thoroughly shaken, the chances are excellent that the thickener is wax. The heavy-bodied type that does not use wax will generally continue to flow evenly. This is a really superior paint remover.

When you shop for a remover, purchase only *top-quality, nonflammable, heavy-bodied paint remover*. This is the most efficacious, the least expensive, and the least dangerous type of paint remover in the liquid-solvent class. *It will not burn wood*. By reading the labels on the cans, you will find such a paint remover, particularly in a reliable paint store or hardware shop. This remover will have enough speed, enough clinging quality, enough sustaining power, and as much solvent power as you can get in this classification. Its ingredients will be mainly a mixture of methylene chloride, alcohol, and thickening agents. It will have a natural built-in safety factor against creating fire hazards plus a much lower human toxicity rating due to the presence of methylene chloride. If this remover gets on the skin, it will smart noticeably, which acts as an instant warning signal. Wash it off immediately with cold water and all will be well again. Compare on the chart on page 63 the toxicity ratings of benzol, and other common paint remover ingredients that are used in most liquid paint removers as solvents, with methylene chloride. You will find you can tolerate twenty times more methylene chloride than benzol (my own feeling is that humans cannot really tolerate benzol at all). Figures opposite the name of the chemical indicate how many parts of chemical mixed with one million parts of air can be tolerated safely. This is the maximum concentration tolerable. Those asterisked are the solvents most commonly found in liquid paint removers. Let there be no mystery or magic in any can from now on. These are reliable figures by which to judge.

TOXICITY RATINGS

*Benzol	25 parts
*Propylene Dichloride	75 "
Chloroform	100 "
Turpentine	100 "
*Methanol (alcohol type)	200 "
*Toluol	200 "
*Xylol or Xylene	200 "
*Methyl Ethyl Keytone	250 "
*Isopropyl Alcohol	400 "
Gasolene or Kerosene	500 "
Mineral Spirits (paint thinner)	500 "
*Methylene Chloride	500 "

Several toxicity charts even rate the recommended methylene chloride as high as 1000 parts, making it actually safer than kerosene, gasolene, isopropyl alcohol (rubbing alcohol), mineral spirits (paint thinner), or turpentine, which is so freely used in the home. Regardless of any difference in the toxicity charts, you can safely employ a paint remover in the lower reaches of the toxicity range. May I suggest that you copy this chart on a card and carry it with you for ready reference when you shop for paint removers?

Getting the Most for Your Money

As I have indicated elsewhere, no magic or miracles must be expected to flow from any commercial liquid-solvent paint remover can. There has been little change or development in this product over the past several decades, so far as paint-cutting efficiency is concerned. The action, application, and general nature is about the same as it was in 1910. The only improvements have been in thickeners, the addition of methylene chloride for nonflammability, and the addition of water-rinsing types which are too expensive for whatever doubtful additional benefits they may offer. Most of the brands now on the market still incorporate the solvents mentioned earlier and practically all of the slightly lower-priced flammable brands—both liquid and semi-paste types—give no benefits beyond those found in similar paint removers made many years ago.

There are four basic types of liquid paint removers sold in metal cans at paint or hardware stores and offered for your consideration.

Highly Flammable Liquid Type—lowest prices but contain wax and often very toxic benzol. Runs and evaporates very quickly and therefore impractical.

Flammable Cream or Semi-Paste Type—middle priced but at extremely high cost to user because of cheaper solvents and wax loading.

Water-Rinsing Nonflammable Type—sold at very high prices, and water-rinsing factor often not strong enough to be practical.

Heavy-Bodied Nonflammable Type—high priced but the most economical with the water-rinsing formula in this book.

Lowest-priced removers will invariably be the thin watery kinds that are *highly flammable*, most toxic, and evaporate quickly, penetrating only thin finishes. They are disappointing if thick layers are to be taken off. The middle-priced brands are mostly highly flammable or flammable and labels display the words "cream," "semi-paste," or "thick-type." They are generally not benzol-type, but use somewhat less volatile solvents such as toluol, toluene, xylol, etc. They will remain "wet" longer due to the heavier loading of wax or a waxlike substance. Because wax is not a solvent—in fact, wax may rise to the surface quickly, once the remover is spread, forming there a barrier against the evaporation of the fast-evaporating solvents—there is reason to hope that the "wetness" will allow solvents to penetrate more deeply.

In the higher-priced reliable brands you should be getting *nonflammable* removers that should contain 70 per cent or more of the methylene chloride (nonflammable) solvent. Some brands may be designated as "semi-paste" and are what we call "heavy-bodied" because of their viscosity, making a thicker, heavier, and slower-flowing liquid. As I have indicated previously, this should not be due to wax but to the presence of methyl cellulose, a good thickener. There are two ways to be sure what the thickener may be:

1. Chill the can to 40 degrees F. as suggested on page 62.

2. Pick up the can in the store and heft it in comparison with a similar-sized remover of another brand. A wax-thickened remover in the semi-paste category will usually weigh less than the methyl-cellulose-thickened type. The difference in weight is great enough to be perceived easily; it may be as much as 40 per cent. Wax is a lightweight substance so that a quart can of the cheaper wax-type remover would weigh about two pounds, while the quality cellulose-type would weigh closer to three pounds. In gallon sizes the wax-type will weigh less than eight pounds; the cellulose-type will be about eleven pounds. If you judge the weights, you will be able to choose the better kind. But

possibly you might want to try both kinds for yourself.

There are other factors to consider. Don't lose money and make more work by allowing too rapid and wasteful evaporation. Work on paint-stripping in cool temperatures, in draftless but well-ventilated spots. Hot, breezy, or sunny areas cause rapid deterioration and quick evaporation of the paint remover.

What Is Removed by a Liquid-Solvent Remover?

The answer is nothing, absolutely nothing concerned in stripping off old finishes. They will soften or wrinkle up old finishes and that is about all; you must do the removing. It is up to you to take off the temporarily liquified old finish—which is the operation so often referred to as the "big mess" or "sludge budging." I recall two elderly ladies who decided to join the "do-it-yourself festivities." They chose to remove the varnish from the flooring of a long unused bedroom and purchased two gallons of liquid paint remover. Most of it was applied to the floor and the two ladies locked the door and tiptoed away. Each day they silently peeped into the room, but with increasing dismay. The "big mess" was still there after two weeks, and after firmly putting away their hopes of going to heaven without once joining the working classes, they sent their chauffeur back to the paint dealer with a stiff and angry note which spoke of fraud. This immediately caused a furor. Alexander Graham Bell would have been surprised at the speed with which this message was sent to the top echelons. Explanations and demonstrations were given, the merits of liquid paint remover were revealed, and the world cooled off again. But what was mainly shown was that the solvent had evaporated, leaving a crackled, messy old finish topped with a heavy smear of wax. This brings us to the point of the discussion: a liquid paint remover is really a paint *softener;* human elbow grease is the paint *remover.*

Invent an Easy Paint Remover

If you can find a really easy way to make old paint go away there is the opportunity of a lifetime awaiting you. I can give you a head start on the problem by telling you about all the other means that man has devised so far; but maybe you already know them from experience.

The electrically heated scraper . . . the blowtorch . . . the electric sander . . . the hand scraper . . . the hand sander . . . the sandblaster . . . the high-pressure water system . . . the ultrasonic vibration method . . . and the gas chamber.

They all have their drawbacks. The electrically heated scraper will soften up thick paint, but although it can be used on clapboards with success, it cannot be recommended for stripping paint from furniture or anything else made of fine woods which will show under a varnish coat. The same is true of the blowtorch, which has the obvious additional drawback of its danger of setting things on fire. The electric belt sander, the vibrating sander, and even the hand sander may be used to wear away paint but they are most impractical for use on furniture. The hand scraper—either the sharp metal blade or the piece of broken glass often recommended—is also not recommended for it often produces regrettable results. How can we be convinced that weeks of our lives should be spent scraping down an old rocking chair with glass or a metal blade? We do not relish the thought, either, of mixing our blood with the wood stain! I have seen people doing both of these things—scraping a chair down with glass (it took all winter) and losing blood. A good paint remover could have done the job in half an hour.

Sandblasters have been used on the sidewalls of large brick or masonry structures and tried out for furniture-stripping. In the latter instance, the results were so bad I hate to talk about them. Sidewalls have also been stripped with expensive high-pressure water apparatus, but five thousand or more pounds of pressure per square inch seems too much for a thick piece of wood. A chair might just disappear! I have also heard about removing finish from electronic parts by ultrasonic equipment, but I hardly think this will amount to a boom in the furniture-stripping business for a long time to come.

So what is left? What can you think of? It is reported that paint disappears quite rapidly in city smogs; is that an idea? How about a gas chamber for tables—with some closure for the furniture after the paint remover has been applied to prevent evaporation until the gas had done its work? This idea has been tried with small plastic bags, too, but plastic sheeting—the kind we know about, anyhow—would allow fumes and gases to escape.

What will the new means be—chemical, or mechanical? If you can think of one that is really effective, and cheap, you can give the paint remover business a much needed boost—and get rich at the same time.

Some Other Chemical Removers

LYE AND WATER. Not all chemical removers are of recent date. Lye and water is a really powerful paint remover and it is inexpensive. But lye-and-water mixes have extremely serious faults and they *cannot* be recommended. Lye is so corrosive that it will not only dissolve paint but also almost everything else it comes in contact with—your clothing, your skin, your eyes and, of course, your furniture. Some people, knowing the destroying qualities of lye, will use it as a "hot" mix: a can full of lye to a quart of very hot water, the lye being poured slowly into the water. It can then be applied with a rag on a stick, if you can make absolutely sure that a splash will not get on you or your clothes—or anything else worthwhile. The mixture must be worked in a warm temperature and it is really too runny for most uses. If lye and water could somehow be put into a controllable paste, so that it would not splash or run, it might be recommended for stripping down thick paint layers.

TRISODIUM PHOSPHATE was used by the old professional strippers with their hot dipping tanks. Some mixed this chemical with potash, another chemical so extremely caustic it is similar to lye. Also, it has been mixed with metasilicate and soda ash. A saturated water solution of trisodium phosphate, called commonly TSP, used in a temperature between very warm and hot, will dissolve paint before your eyes. It is not particularly dangerous, but unfortunately the soaking of hot water penetrates so deeply that the furniture is likely to be ruined before the paint leaves.

While I do not recommend TSP for stripping, I most certainly advocate its use for general heavy-duty cleaning and for an "after wash" in the stripping procedure detailed on page 75. Remember it, for it will come in handy.

COMMERCIAL AMMONIA has been suggested at various times as a remover for old milk, or refractory, paints. These were frequently the original finishes on many antique pieces. There are some claims that it will remove varnish. I make no recommendations on either score for commercial ammonia is terribly dangerous (which may be why you cannot buy it through common channels). The fumes are unbearable; I hardly dare to guess how those other fellows used it, unless they were equipped with heavy rubber wear and a gas mask.

SAL SODA has been mentioned, too. Not long ago I read: "Bear in mind that paint remover is never used on an antique, except when the piece has been plastered with layer upon layer of paint. The professional restorers usually work with sal soda concentrated and dissolved in water."

Personally I have never had any luck with sal soda, but I do have an idea of what the writer was trying to say. Certain collectors or museums are very particular about their valuable pieces—they have reason to be: a certain chest-on-chest was valued at over $40,000 and a certain sofa sold for over $25,000. But most of us do not operate on this level of the economy and our aim is merely to make articles look as we think they should, for our home—smooth, clean, colorful, and functional.

Regardless of the fact that simpler, easier methods have been devised, people still wield primitive and archaic tools, still work harder than they need to. A large city newspaper recently carried this headline: FIRST JOB IN RESTORING—GET THE FINISH OFF. The lengthy article went into much detail about hand scraping, using various sizes and kinds of steel scrapers with only this reference to stripping in a small final paragraph, which we quote in full: "As for using the varnish removers, directions should be followed and plenty of patience exercised by the doer."

Our work would surely never be done if we resorted to steel blades; furthermore, I don't believe the work would ever be done right. "As for using the varnish remover ——" there is a lot more to learn about chemical removers than what is said on labels with their brief, terse directions. I think the author misplaced the word "patience"—it belonged there with those steel scrapers. I prefer a higher level of safety, not to mention efficiency, than data from rules that might have been applicable in 1901.

How About a Powder Remover?

A powder method has been developed by a small chemical company not yet identified with the big paint remover manufacturers. When mixed with water, it will set in a smooth, brushable cream and when applied will efficiently remove thick layers of paint that are still so much of a barrier to the regular liquid paint removers. This product may prove to be the best answer to the tough problem of removing paint. I have used it many times in test after test and believe this product is worthy of the following report:

Hundreds of tests have been made and some professional paint-strippers for furniture as well as master painters report excitedly about pleasing results. The powder is intended for the removal of thick layers of paint—it is not intended for removing thin layers of shellac, varnish, or lacquers, although it will dissolve shellac and varnish. The makers agree that the better way of taking off thin, clear-type finishes is still with the popular liquid paint removers. Any demonstration or test of both types of removers would convince anyone, however, of powder's superiority over liquids when applied to thick paints, actually dissolving heavy layers of paint so that they can be washed away with water. Powder is free from the dangers cited for most liquids, is entirely nontoxic, does not give off fumes or gases. One can work with it in close quarters without fear of toxic inhalation. It can cause irritation if it is allowed to touch the skin or body, but water will wash it off quickly and easily and care can be exercised to keep from touching it. It will take a bit longer to apply a thick, even coating on rounded surfaces, which is a drawback, of course. But on flat surfaces it is almost ideal.

If there are thick coatings of paint on country furniture, flooring, walls, ceilings, outdoor sideboarding, clapboards, wooden boats, or metal articles—with the exception of aluminum—powder can be recommended for all as a remover. It will not burn or destroy woods like the chemicals mentioned previously. It goes right on dissolving layer after layer of old paints until eight to ten layers have been penetrated. As long as it remains water-moist and the temperature is about 65 degrees F. or warmer it will work well. In fact, the warmer the day, the better it works. I was making a powder test on several heavily coated antique doors in a northern Vermont house when the temperature zoomed to 98 degrees. The old-style paints I was removing were the sort upon which the liquid paint removers had little effect and there were about a dozen coats in thick layers. In less than thirty minutes I washed right down to bare wood; the hot day gave me the extra help.

Another test came through a master painter who had a contract to strip paint from a large house and then repaint completely. He was unable to use a blow torch because of a town ordinance and he knew that liquid paint removers would be fantastically expensive. Fortunately it was warm weather when he located and tested a powder product. Results were so good on the test area that he began mixing five-gallon batches on the spot. They enabled him to strip the paint with the greatest possible ease and at the lowest cost. Professional furniture-strippers are using it with success, too. In their shallow tanks, about a foot in depth, they mix large quantities and then roll in heavily painted old furniture for a fast and uniform coating of remover. If the temperature is right, twenty minutes to an hour is the general time allowed for complete dissolving and a wash-down afterward with water. Powder can be recommended for furniture with heavy coatings of paints as well as for fine antique houses with their fine wide pine wainscoting, flooring, and paneling. At the time of writing, this product has not yet found its way into the standard hardware or paint markets, but it is listed among the sources at the end of the book (see page 206).

We have come to the end of the briefing on the various paint removers available. This background knowledge should greatly enhance your success in future refinishing and restoration. The next step is to learn what sort of finish you will be trying to remove.

9. STRIPPING OFF THE FINISH

"Stripping" is the word used in the restoring and refinishing business for the process of taking off easily, quickly, and as safely as possible the accumulation of finishes—shellac, varnish, and lacquer, as well as coatings of oil paints and enamels. There is a way to go about it to insure success and if the suggestions offered here are followed, you will be sure to have that success.

First of all, wear old clothing. And use heavy, cloth-lined rubber gloves to protect your hands not only from the dirt and gooey paint and varnish as it is removed, but also from the harsh effects of the removers on the skin. Some people are more affected than others by the chemicals, but why take chances at all? Wear protective eyeglasses to prevent splashes from entering the eyes. Choose a work area that is well ventilated, cool, out of the sun, and with no drafts or wind currents.

Remove drawer pulls and other removable hardware before you begin to strip the furniture and set them aside for a later bath of paint remover. Place the piece of furniture where you can work easily on it—either on the floor if it is a large piece or on a low table if it is a smaller-sized one. Now you are ready to begin, so make up all the mixtures you will need and assemble your paint remover and whatever will be needed to do the job properly.

First is the paint remover. Shake the can with its contents of heavy-bodied, nonflammable paint remover to mix thoroughly all of the ingredients. When you unscrew the cap, twist it only slightly and wait a moment to allow any air pressure built up to escape, once the seal is broken. Pour out a cupful or more of remover into a coffee can or other wide, low receptacle. Use a soft inexpensive or old brush to apply the remover and *flow* it on. Do not brush it back and forth as you would if you were painting—you are now *removing* paint. The object is to flow on the remover as thickly as possible and *let it remain to do its work*. In about five to ten minutes, use a blunt instrument such as a putty knife or an old table knife to make a test scraping. You will see how far the remover has penetrated through the finish. Thin coatings of clear finishes will probably be completely loosened from the surface by now. If not, check again in another ten minutes; if the finish has not been loosened by twenty minutes from the first check-scraping, apply another coat of remover. It is not necessary to scrape off the old finish. The effective agents of the liquid formula have evaporated after doing their work. More will be needed to complete the separation of the finish from the wood. Some finishes bubble up, others may crinkle, but some merely become soft.

While the finish is softening, mix up the washing-off liquid. This is made from *trisodium phosphate* (TSP). Use a cupful of TSP to two quarts of very hot water and about four tablespoonfuls of a strong laundry detergent. Mix well in an old pail. Add three to four quarts of cold water so that the washing-off solution will be cool. *Never wash down with a warm or hot solution*. If you are unable to procure TSP, you may use any heavy-duty household cleaner, but add a greater quantity of laundry detergent.

Before washing down, lay down an absorbent pad of old newspapers several papers thick—the thicker the better—so that you can take care of any sloppiness that may result and also clean up more easily and quickly once the job is done. Some craftsmen like to lay the papers down before they flow on the remover, so as to avoid having to move the piece while it is full of sticky paint.

Washing Down

Now that the paint remover has done its work the finish has been completely softened and if there have been a number of coats, there will be a thick "sludge," as it is called, to be removed. Begin the process by using two or three pads of coarse #3 steel wool, dipping them into the pail of solution to keep them constantly saturated. Pick up as much as possible of the sludge each time you rub, then wash it out in the solution. On flat surfaces, *always work with the grain of the wood,* to prevent cross-scratching. On chair legs, rungs, and spindles, press the steel wool pad around the turned surface, and lightly but firmly exert pressure as you push the pad up and down.

When most of the heavy sludge has been removed, use a large sponge or a pad of rough cloth in the same way that you used the steel wool. Always, with the steel wool or with the sponge, work with the wood grain and exert a light but firm pressure that is constant. When all the old finish has been removed, wipe the surfaces with an old turkish towel or other soft cloth to dry it quickly. Sometimes you will need another washdown or a stronger solution. Every stripping job has problems. No overall advice can cover every one.

If the finish consisted of only one or two layers of paint, or if there was only a thin layer of clear finish—varnish, shellac, or lacquer—you need use only a sponge or rough cloth for the washing down. On very thick coatings of paint, using a liquid paint remover, you may wish to apply the remover and after it has done as much as it can, push off with a *dull* putty or spackling knife as much of the sludge as possible and remove it. After this reapply the remover and let it work, then wash down as detailed above. If all of the finish did not come off when using the final procedure just detailed, then either the remover was not of a good quality or the finish was of a type that liquid paint removers could not sink through. See page 71, where a solution to this problem is suggested.

Carvings and Deep Moldings

Where a piece is ornamented with deeply carved moldings or ornamental carvings, steel wool may not remove all of the sludge from deep cuts and crevices. Use an old toothbrush, a vegetable brush, or other stiff-bristled brush to clean out the sludge, repeating the application of remover if necessary to clean out more finish. When washed, the carvings should be as clean and free from finish as the tops or other flat surfaces.

Although the TSP washing-off liquid should complete the work and give you a completely clean surface, if you have used one of the liquid paint removers which contains wax (and I suggest you reread the section on choosing a remover to refresh your memory at this point) there may be a considerable residue of wax left after the paint has been removed. This residue will interfere with the application of the new finish and prevent the perfect job you wish to achieve. You can be certain to remove all wax and grease by simply wiping the piece, once it has dried out from the washdown, with a clean old turkish towel saturated with mineral spirits (obtainable from paint stores as paint thinner). Keep folding the cloth as you wipe down the piece to offer a new surface of cloth with fresh mineral spirits to pick up the wax. You will also be removing the silicones found in many polishing preparations today which will interfere with a good smooth refinishing job.

The New Washdown Method

Twenty years or so ago I may have been the first to perform paint removal by washing down furniture in this way, but many people have now taken up this easy and safe method. I have never experienced any bad results. I always protect my clothes by using old ones, protect my hands with rubber gloves, and I have had great success. Yet articles are written all the time which advocate the outmoded old methods, recommending scraping off the finish when loosened (which I feel may scratch or mar the wood surfaces) and making a hard job of it. Some say, "You will raise the grain of the wood if you wash with water," or, "Using a water-rinsing remover will burn the wood." Still others say, "You will damage the veneer or the patina." I think I have proved many times, and to anybody's satisfaction, that modern veneering can stand up to a water washing, and sound old veneering can, too. In a few instances and with certain woods, the grain may be slightly roughened, but in the final sanding down that will be taken care of anyhow. If the patina is in the finish, it will be removed, of course, but if it is true patina, it will be in the wood, so nothing is lost. As to water-rinsing paint removers or the water-washing solution's burning the wood, I have never found a brand with which this happened and I have experimented with about every known brand that is offered to the nonprofessional refinisher.

Exceptions to the Rule

1. If you have only a small flat surface to strip, most of the sludge can be gently pushed off with a blunt, broad spackle knife. The rest can be mopped up and removed with a cloth saturated with paint thinner or alcohol.

2. On very valuable antiques, and particularly those with loosening veneer or inlay, other methods than washing down should be employed. The method detailed under No. 1 might be used, with great care to keep from breaking or destroying the veneer.

3. Small, uncomplicated articles such as picture frames need not be washed down with water but can be wiped up with paint thinner, alcohol, or turpentine.

Always wash out the steel wool pads and sponges or cloths thoroughly or dispose of them after allowing them to dry. Never store cloths that contain any paint remover chemicals. They might cause trouble if used again for another purpose.

Knobs and hardware can be stripped with paint remover, washed off with the water mixture, or wiped with paint thinner, alcohol, or turpentine.

If the methods above were used, you are now ready to begin the refinishing of the pieces. If there were thicker layers of paint, or you encountered other problems, then you may have to use other methods, such as those which follow.

A Little Fun with Modern Chemistry

We have suggested a TSP (trisodium phosphate) and laundry detergent mix, or a heavy-duty household cleaner and laundry detergent mix. The TSP will supply the best dissolving or cutting action, while the laundry detergent will supply emulsification properties.

Beside the cutting action, you need the emulsifying action, similar to the emulsification properties that are put into the very expensive water-wash, nonflammable paint removers. You may find a better mix for your work with a little simple experimenting.

I have used some modern dishwashing detergents with

success, too. They are the thickish emulsions in plastic bottles, such as Lux, Joy, and others. So you can see for yourself: make a mix of one-half cupful of paint thinner, two tablespoonsful of water, and one tablespoonful of Lux pink dishwashing liquid. You will have made a most wonderful heavy-duty hand cleaner for your home workshop almost instantly and certainly you will see how easy it is to mix oil and water—and remove paint remover sludge!

Others have used the detergent properties found in Wisk, Top Job, Ajax, Mr. Clean, etc. Also, washdown mixes have been made with Tide, Cheer, All, and Dash.

In every case, however, I hope that the other part of the mix can be TSP; in the kind of work we are doing, the cutting and dissolving action will be better than if you use such household cleaners as Oakite, Spic & Span, or Soilax.

Stripping Thick Coats of Paint

The commercial liquid paint removers will eventually remove most paints and thick coatings, but there is a better product now available for this particular purpose. This is the powder type of paint stripper referred to on page 71, not generally known to the public because it is not yet widely distributed to paint and hardware stores. There are but two firms at the present time who make this product and they are listed at the end of the book (page 206) for those who wish to pursue the subject and purchase this remover, if it is not locally available.

Some professionals now use considerable quantities of this product. It is most useful where there are multiple layers of common oil paints or the old refractory or milk paints. The removers are advertised in small region magazines and trade papers catering to the antiques trades and the collector. You may see them advertised and be able to buy them by mail order, or you can write to the companies listed at the end of the book to procure them or learn of local distributors.

These removers work in a different way. They are complex alkaline mixtures that actually dissolve the thick layers of paint and save the arduous labor of scraping, formerly the only recourse. There are no fumes or vapors, the mixture is not toxic, and there is no fire hazard from using this method. The old finish is merely washed off with water and a sponge. If the wood darkens—this may occur on some woods, oak, for example—washing immediately after the rinsing with strong vinegar or oxalic acid will generally restore the light color quickly. Brushing on a thick coating of the remover will cause six to ten layers to dissolve within a half hour if the remover is kept damp or moist with water, for there is no fast evaporation of the remover as is the case with commercial liquid types. Occasionally as much as one to two hours may be required for very stubborn cases, or for very thick layers of paint.

Provide yourself with old cloths, heavy rubber gloves, and protective eyeglasses, as for any stripping operation. Then proceed according to the manner outlined. For washing down, water only is needed for this kind of remover, and if you are able to put the piece outdoors, a hosing down and a quick drying off with soft absorbent cloths will cut the time and labor to practically nothing.

Bleaching the Wood

If there are stains of ink, sap, dye, oil, or grease on the piece, or if the wood has darkened unduly, the wood may be bleached to lighten the shade and also to rid the wood of the stains. This is not a common undertaking in the home workshop and I must emphasize that it usually involves employing some dangerous or at least potentially dangerous chemicals. But it is sometimes of prime importance to the success of restoration, so I shall try to make the information understandable and as safe to use as possible.

Strong bleaching is done with powerful alkalines that react against strong acids. For a test: Dissolve a half-teaspoonful of lye crystals in a quart of water and two tablespoonfuls of oxalic acid crystals in a different quart of very hot water, using glass or enamel receptacles for each. We now have an alkaline mixture (lye) and an acid mixture (oxalic acid). With a piece of cheesecloth tied to a stick, apply a little of the lye mixture to a small area of the wood or to the spot to be bleached. Let it stand for a minute or two. The wood will darken, growing darker and darker, particularly if it is oak. Now use another cheesecloth tied to a stick and apply some of the oxalic acid mixture over the same spot. The wood will lighten and the spot will often disappear. Stubborn spots and stains may take two or more applications. The wood and the spot may even be lighter than it was as bare wood! Paint stores can supply both lye and oxalic acid.

A word of caution: Lye is a very powerful corrosive and therefore dangerous. Read the labels carefully. Oxalic acid is poisonous when taken internally, so exercise every care if you use it.

Paint stores and sometimes hardware shops also sell a packaged, two-bottle, stronger bleaching preparation. These generally contain a weak solution of lye in water in one bottle with the other bottle containing a commercial peroxide. Note that this is *commercial peroxide,* not the 3 per cent peroxide solution sold at drugstores for other purposes. Because it is a somewhat unstable mixture of about 20 per cent to 30 per cent peroxide, it is highly dangerous. *Eyes and skin must be protected from it.* Use it only if it is absolutely necessary and be very careful.

Another bleach sometimes used is the common kitchen bleach. Read *all* of the label. You will probably find that it is a weak solution of sodium hypochlorite. Vapors released are not only objectionable but are also sickening to many people. Maintain good ventilation and be careful if you use it. I do not recommend it; it is not only weak, but it is also likely to run and be uncontrollable. Again, it should not be used because it can actually disintegrate the top wood fibers and really "raise the grain," as many people claim water-washing alone can do.

To sum up, the best bleaches or wood lighteners are oxalic acid solutions. Remember that they are internally poisonous and exercise every care. Wear rubber gloves. Work in a well-ventilated spot and always make sure to keep oxalic acid solutions away from the mouth. Do not allow oxalic acid to dry on wood. If, when it is nearly dry, the color has not lightened sufficiently, apply another coat of the oxalic acid solution. If allowed to dry on the wood, oxalic acid will reform into crystals, dangerous to inhale as you smooth the wood, and also likely to interfere with the refinishing coats. Therefore wash down well with a mixture of water and household ammonia—two tablespoons to a quart of water—or with plain warm water.

For lightening wood where a stain to simulate mahogany has been applied previously, as on Colonial and Early American antiques, use a wash of full-strength household ammonia. When it dries, wash off with water.

A bleaching procedure that can do little harm and is mild, often giving the wood tone desired, is a variation of the oxalic acid method. Substitute for the oxalic acid solution a citric acid solution. A quarter-pound of citric acid crystals (probably available through your druggist) dissolved in one to two quarts of water will make the proper washing solution. Citric acid is used by the ton in the soft drink industry, so it must be safe. Tartaric or phosphoric acid are also suggested by some for use as a washing solution, but I have no formula to offer for them. A general citric acid wash may suffice.

If the piece in question is too deeply stained to be revived by bleaching or if the process is too much for you to attempt, consider using a painted finish that will cover up the blemish and make it acceptable for use. A coat or two of semi-gloss or gloss paint or enamel will do the trick. A painted piece will often enliven a room and give it the value of contrast, and painted pieces have an honorable history as you will find in reading about antiques and observing them in museums and shops. Not all furniture need be finished in its natural wood grain or even its natural color. If discolorations are not too dark or too deep, and you do not wish to paint the piece, apply a slightly darker stain than you had planned to use. This will disguise the blemish and no one need ever know the stain or discoloration was there.

10. REPAIRING ANTIQUES

If you examine furniture and make careful selections, repairing need not be a major part of restoration. If there is a piece which is exactly what you have been looking for and the bargain is too great to resist, however, some repair may be necessary before the piece can be refinished and used. Unless you are an experienced craftsman, major repairs are best left to a cabinetmaker or someone who knows how to do the job properly. Just be sure that in the repairing process he does not "restore" the piece beyond what is needed and destroy the beauty as well as the value by using the wrong kinds of woods, or by failing to copy exactly what must be replaced, preferably in old woods.

If the problem is the usual one—general looseness of the joints and squeaks—this can usually be taken care of by using one of two kinds of glue and possibly a little ordinary string. For all ordinary repairs where glue alone is needed, I always use a white glue, such as Elmer's Glue-All or Weldwood Presto-Set Glue, both of which come in a plastic bottle with a dispenser top.

If the problems are greater—repairs and tightening-up which will undergo considerable stress and strain—these are best repaired with epoxy glue which comes in two tubes that must be mixed together for use. The epoxy will make a very strong repair but it does not dry or harden quickly, and must remain undisturbed for twenty-four hours in order to set properly. Some epoxy glues dry out opaque-white like writing paper and these are best avoided, although on painted furniture this may not matter too much. Look for the clear type which will dry out colorless, so that repairs are as unnoticeable as possible.

Common store string, the white cotton kind, is handy to have in the home workshop. If wear has loosened a wood screw and it does not hold properly or if there is a drawer pull with a shank that has worn the hole in the wood so that it wobbles, wrap a short length of string around the screw or the metal shank, load it with white glue and reinsert in the hole. Let it set for two hours or so and it will be tight again for a long, long time.

If a chair or table has loose joints, first check the undersides for bolts and screws. Sometimes they merely need tightening. Screws may sometimes be replaced by screws the same length but fatter. If nails were used by a lazy repairman, pull them out, fill the joint with epoxy glue and then squeeze the joint together, removing excess glue. Tie a rope around the entire piece or place it on the side and weight it to hold the joint firmly together. Leave it for at least a day so that the glue can firm up.

REPAIRING RUNGS, SPINDLES, AND SPOKES.   Pull out of the socket all of these which are loose or squeaky, scrape off and sand away the glue, but do not take off any of the wood. Re-glue, using epoxy if it is a stress joint, replace and hold tightly for a few minutes to firm it in the socket, then weight the joint and allow to dry for a day. If you cannot get a rung out of its socket without doing damage, it is possible to insert a small round dowel peg or whittled oak peg or a nail from which the head has been cut to hold it in place. Drill a hole of similar diameter to the peg or nail through the leg and rung from the side, coat the peg or nail (which must be shorter than the depth of the hole) with glue, and insert it, pushing it in so that it fits snugly. When the repair is dry, fill the shallow hole left above the peg or nail with stick shellac, softened in alcohol.

STICKING DRAWERS. Frequently rubbing the runners with wax or a cake of soap will lubricate them enough to make them run smoothly. If the draw is slanted or if the runners are worn down or broken, however, you may have to replace the runners. Strips of soft pine are best for this and strips cut to match but slightly larger than the old strips (to compensate for wear) or complete, if runners are broken, should be used. Epoxy glue can be used and may be preferable to using fine thin box nails inserted through small holes drilled through the wood. If the drawer is slanted and out of shape, it will not pull properly. Force it back into a perfect right-angled shape and glue the loose joint that has allowed it to spring out of line. You may have to take the joint apart, scrape off the old glue and re-glue it, but it will repay the effort. Keep the drawer clamped or set in the proper right-angle shape for at least two hours if white glue is used, twenty-four hours if epoxy is used.

DENTS. If dents are not too deep, they may be raised to the surface in most cases. First wet the dented area (the finish must, of course, have been removed from this area beforehand), and let the wood soak up the water. It may be enough to swell the wood cells and bring the surface back to normal when it dries. If not, wet the wood again, lay a woolen cloth over the soaked area around the dent, and apply a fairly hot flatiron. The water in the wood cells will turn to steam, expanding the wood cells and making them rise to the surface. Some people use a wet cloth, in addition to wetting and soaking the wood, when applying the iron. If the first application does not raise the dent, several applications may be required to do the job. If the dent has broken the fibers of the wood and sharp edges are left, however, it is probably useless to try this method. Fill the dent with wood putty and stain the patched-in dent to match the wood so that it will not show in the finished job.

DEEP SCRATCHES.   First sandpaper the scratch lightly and examine it. If it is shallow, only fine sanding along the scratch line may be needed. Apply a matching stain and, when it is dry, touch up the scratch with full-bodied varnish. If the scratch is minor, it may need only to be rubbed lightly and gently with a paste of very fine pumice mixed with boiled linseed oil. Clean with mineral spirits, rub with a dry clean cloth, then apply varnish colored to match by adding a drop or two of matching stain color to a small quantity of varnish. When the scratch is wide and deep, it is best to use a sawdust-and-glue filler. This is a paste made of fine sawdust and epoxy, used rather dry, not too much glue to the amount of sawdust, that is. Press it into the deep scratch and level it as best you can, then allow a little to bulge above the surface. When it is thoroughly dry, sand it down level with the top, using a block of wood and sanding paper or emery cloth. The entire panel or surface may have to be refinished if the scratch is a bad one or if there are several scratches. Of course some antiquers feel that scratches and gouges give character and distinction and they do not like to renew and repair too much.

On wide cracks or gouges or deep dents not otherwise reparable, fill with colored stick shellac. This can be bought in several colors—light brown, dark brown, tan, etc.—at paint stores. Use a hot soldering iron or a hot metal rod (a large nail held in the gas flame of the stove with a pair of pliers might do) to melt some of the stick shellac. Allow drops of it to fall into the prepared hole or gouge as it melts, gradually filling it up. Do not hurry or you may make air bubbles. Fill until it is a little above the surface level and, when the shellac has cooled, it can be smoothed off a little with the hot iron, being careful not to scorch the wood, if it is lumpy. Let it cool completely, then with sanding block and sanding paper apply an even pressure to the area and sand down to surface level. If the shellac has not matched, you can match the varnish by adding a little stain as detailed above. Touch up the area and let it dry.

After all repairs of scratches, give a paste-wax finish over the entire surface.

SMALL MISSING PIECE.   If a small piece is missing, such as a bit of the edge of a pie-crust table top or the corner of a drawer front, repair it with a paste of fine sawdust and epoxy glue, building up the hole with the paste or filling out the missing area. Use twice as much sawdust as glue for the paste. Overfill somewhat and pack in the paste with the fingers to shape it. Allow the fill to dry and harden for a day or two, then it can be roughly filed to shape it and finally shaped and smoothed with emery cloth. This kind of patch cannot be stained with wood stains, so that finishing with a colored varnish is the only recourse. With skill, a repair can. be made that is almost perfect and blended to match so that it can hardly be detected.

CRACKED THIN WOOD.   Sometimes a thin wood panel is cracked all the way through and replacing it or taking it out to glue it would entail too much work or it might be impossible. Nails, screws, or another piece of wood are equally out of the question. On the inside, or if it is a panel visible from both sides in the piece in question, fix a piece of waxed paper behind the crack with masking tape. Lay the panel horizontal with the crack open-side upward. If the crack is thin and narrow, fill it with epoxy glue. If it is wide, use the mixture of fine sawdust and epoxy glue detailed above. Allow it to dry for a day or two, smooth it off with emery cloth, and refinish with the colored varnish mixed to match. The crack will be much less noticeable and the wood less likely to dry out and crack again.

CHECKED CLEAR FINISH.   If the old finish seems to have a million tiny cracks in it, this is essentially what they are. These cracks are usually caused by the incompatibilities of tension in the various layers of finish. One layer contracts or expands more than the other layers with temperature changes, not with light as some people say. If the piece stands in sunlight, however, there is bound to be a great change in the temperature and checking may be inevitable. If you buy an antique piece with a checked finish, you can sometimes mitigate the trouble (although you cannot elimi-nate it entirely) by rubbing down the old surfaces with #000 or #00 steel wool and then polishing the surfaces with brown paste wax. There may be enough of an improvement to warrant bypassing a complete stripping of the old finish and refinishing the piece.

DIRTY, OILY, GREASY STAINS ON WOOD.   After stripping, you may find stains of this sort. Wash them several times with mineral spirits on a clean cloth and allow them to dry each time between washings. If this does not eliminate the stains, try the following: Buy a rug cleaner with a base of wood flour and *trichlorethylene*. Apply a thick coating and allow it to dry out thoroughly. The *trichlorethylene* is a grease solvent, the wood flour is the agent into which the grease will be deposited as the solvent evaporates. The powdered wood can then be brushed away with the grease in it. I have used this with great success on antique wooden ware. Some recommend using wheat flour or cornmeal with carbon tetrachloride mixed with it, but I must caution that "carbon tet" (used in certain cleaners) is very, very toxic and must be used with excellent ventilation. Avoid breathing it or coming into too much contact with it.

VENEER. Blisters often occur in old veneer because they check and allow moisture to get behind them, or because moisture collects under a vase or other object on a surface. The veneer then rises in a blister as it separates from the under wood. This is easily taken care of. Slice carefully down the middle of the blister *with the grain*. Lift each side of the slice in turn with the blade, doing it carefully so that you do not split or break the veneer further. Insert some glue under it—white glue or epoxy—with a thin piece of wood or a razor blade. After both sides have been re-glued, press the veneer down, remove any excess glue squeezed out of the slice, then put a heavy weight on top of several sheets of newspaper over the re-glued part. In a day or two, peel off the newspaper, soak off what you can of what adheres, and sand down the rest or scrape them carefully off with a razor blade.

Raised veneer on corners and edges can be repaired similarly, but there is no need for slicing, as with blisters the edges merely being lifted and glue brushed under with a brush or inserted on thin pieces of wood, if the veneer is loosened only slightly.

Replacing lost veneer is tricky. Often veneered edges or parts of pieces have a few odd patches missing, or the veneer may have been broken off, leaving jagged bits. It is possible to buy veneer at crafts shops but of course you cannot guarantee that the veneer purchased will match in color or grain the veneer that is missing. Nevertheless, nonmatching veneer is better than no veneer. If it is possible to remove some veneer from a less conspicuous part of the piece and glue it in neatly and with as little crack as possible between the pieces, the missing veneer from the other spot can be patched in with nonmatching veneer purchased from a supplier. Always examine antiques to be sure the veneer is intact even if loose. Do not discard any pieces—you will need them for repair.

MISSING RUNG OR LEG.   If you have inherited, bought at auction, or otherwise acquired a chair—be it Chippendale, Hitchcock, or Victorian—that you have not spent much money on, it will pay to replace a leg, a rung, or a spindle that is missing. If you have a craftsman in the home who has a lathe, or if you have in your community some craftsman who will do wood turning, it will pay to have this done to match the missing or broken leg, rung, or spindle. Have them use the same kind of wood, then stain and otherwise work it into harmony with the old piece. You now have a "married" piece, or more properly it might be called a "restored" piece.

OTHER REPAIRS.   While it may be romantic to have an old chair with broken caning, shredded rush-work seats, or broken, imperfect carving, furniture in the home should be for use and anything that interferes with normal use should be replaced or repaired. That was the way things were done in times past as furniture wore out—why not do it now? There are professional caners, people who do good rush work, and craftsmen who can repair carving or match, copy, or repair almost anything—provided you are willing to pay the price. Good workmanship is not cheap these days, but so long as it is *good,* it is worth the price. People get about what they pay for, generally, and a cheap price usually means shoddy workmanship or having to pay all over again to correct the mistakes.

SOME FINAL THOUGHTS.   While I have made every effort
to give the background needed to make repairs, to bleach
out stains, to remove dents and gouges, I must point out that
most scars are honorable wounds in the battle of life and
that they may be very valuable assets on certain old chairs,
tables, and chests. It proves the authenticity of the piece
and spurs one's imagination to speculate on how the gouge
or scratch occurred. How did that inkstain come to be on
that table top or desk? How did that wear on the side of that
chest occur? Why is that chair arm worn on the left side
more than on the right side? Did that gouge come from
moving from one house to another or was it, possibly, the
result of a family fight? You can get a lot of imaginative
dividends if you leave the gouges there—and each piece of
furniture will be a real conversation piece.

Perfection kills pure joy, so let us not erase all the good
and bad from the past. Faultless furniture can never be
found, as the wit and poet Oliver Wendell Holmes (1809–
1894) testified:

> Now in building chaises
> I'll tell you what—
> There is always somewhere
> A weakest spot.

And Sherlock Holmes, the masterful creation of Sir Arthur
Conan Doyle, proved to all the world that all of men's
creations have built-in weaknesses. We must, as intelligently
as possible, and as honestly and cleverly as we can, search
out and repair the weakest spots in our antiques. Once
repaired and mended, they are strong again and will be able
to last into future generations, to be enjoyed and cherished.

11. SMOOTHING WOOD

Just as there is need for a final smoothing and finishing of raw woods in new furniture before the final staining or varnishing takes place, so must refinished furniture be smoothed and prepared for the final refinishing operations. There are some modern aids that will prove useful in this work and cut down on the laborious parts of it. In new-wood work, the use of fillers to close the pores of the *open-grain woods* for the final processes is necessary, as well as the use of sanding or smoothing papers. When furniture is refinished, the leftover effects of the former finish (after the use of commercial paint removers) may be good enough to permit refinishing without the use of fillers. Nevertheless, there are certain woods and certain occasions when filling will be necessary.

The average paint store or hardware shop has a large assortment of various kinds of sanding papers and associated products. Here is this rather confusing array in fairly simple and practical order.

Flint and garnet papers—desirable for smoothing soft woods. Abrasives on a paper backing.

Silicone carbide paper—all-purpose smoothing papers, the only type needed. Abrasives on a paper backing.

Emery cloth—flexible; abrasives on a cloth backing. Good for smoothing rungs, spokes, turnings, etc.

Crocus cloth—very fine abrasives on cloth backing; good for rubbing between coatings.

NOTE: The numbers printed on the backing cloth or paper indicate the coarseness or fineness of the abrasives. The higher the number the finer the abrasive particles will be. The #200 series is coarse to medium; #300, medium; #400, fine; and #500, very fine. Only a small stock of silicone carbide paper in medium and fine grades is ever needed, plus some fine emery cloth for use on rounds.

SMOOTHING FLAT SURFACES. Always be sure to keep the paper flat under even pressure. This can be done easily by wrapping a piece of the paper around a small rectangular block of wood that fits easily into the hand and can be grasped to hold it firmly. *Follow the grain of the wood,* using long sweeping strokes; *never grind across the grain.* Use a coarser grade for the first smoothing, then end with a fine grade.

SMOOTHING RUNGS AND SPOKES. For any curved and uneven areas, use the flexible emery cloth, following the grain—which usually runs the length of the turning—up and down. Tear narrow strips of emery cloth to sand in crevices of the turnings and clean and smooth them.

MACHINE SMOOTHING. Powered machines such as those used by professionals and ardent home craftsmen are useful for large flat areas. The various oscillating and vibrating types of electric sanders are good for this, and if you have a very large quantity of flat surface to smooth, even a belt sander may come in handy. But I doubt that most readers will have so much smoothing to do that they will require such machines. A little hand smoothing of surfaces is probably all that will be necessary for the refinisher, so an investment in an electric machine is not indicated.

Once the wood is stripped of the old finish, if it is found to be very porous, filling is in order if you wish to have the final surface as smooth as glass. This applies to oak and mahogany woods, mostly. There may also be occasional chestnut or walnut pieces that require filling, especially if the wood in the original sawing did not quite go with the natural grain. Wood filler is obtainable in a light natural shade, or it can be purchased in tones that will nearly match the stain you plan to use. Basically, filler is a pasty mass that is rubbed across the grain, filling the pores to the surrounding surface to create a smooth foundation for the final finishes. Directions are simple: Read the label, first of all. Thin the filler as directed, then apply liberally with a brush. Turpentine or mineral spirits is the usual medium for thinning. Fill only a small area at a time, if you are working on a large surface—a small table top can be filled in one operation, for instance. Allow the filler to dry for a short time, ten to twenty minutes, and then, while it is still not quite set, wipe it off *briskly* across the grain with a piece of burlap or other coarse cloth, pushing the filler well down into the pores. After this, wipe *lightly* with the grain to finish it, but be sure to use a light hand so you do not push the filler out of the pores. Allow it to dry for about a day, twenty-four hours at least. Then sand it lightly with the grain to remove any filler that may have adhered to the top of the wood or projected beyond the pores. The function of the filler is merely to fill pores and small cracks and failure to remove any excess may result in a streaked or cloudy effect in the final finish.

The old wood fillers were probably a mixture of three things: ground-up quartz called "silex" or "silica," linseed oil, and a drying agent. A small can of prepared filler can go a long way and the expense is so modest it is not practical to make your own filler. If you have a good deal of filling to be done, it may be better to buy the natural shade, and tint a small quantity for each job according to the color of the wood. Use oil color in the thinning agent, matching or harmonizing the color with yellow-brown, red-brown, or whatever shade the wood is when the finish is removed. Natural is used for new woods and for light-colored woods.

Hard-grained woods are close grained and pores are small. Such woods as pine, birch, maple, and cherry need no filler for this reason. But the coarser-grained woods such as oak, mahogany, and walnut should usually be filled unless the remover has not taken out the original filling.

Shellac acts as a liquid filler for many woods, or for wood that has been filled previously, filling all the pores of close-grained woods and the smaller ones of coarse-grained woods. One or two coats of quick-drying shellac should be enough for most work. You should stain woods to the desired color and shade before the shellac coats. After the shellac has dried, use a fine grade of silicone carbide paper to smooth the surface before applying the finish coats of varnish.

Modern smoothing papers follow a long tradition and the newest of the papers take account of an old technique. When the early craftsman smoothed his woods, he used water as a lubricant; our newest wet-or-dry smoothing papers suggest the same thing. On raw or clear wood the paper should be used in dry form, but when smoothing between finish coats, or when smoothing wood already well sealed, work with the paper on a surface that is wet with water. If your dealer does not stock *silicone carbide wet-or-dry papers* marked as noted here—that is, #200, #300, #400, #500—the papers available may be graded #2/0, #3/0, #4/0, etc., or possibly identified simply as medium, fine, very fine, and so on. You can recognize the grades by eye, of course, judging by the fineness or coarseness of the particles adhering to the backing.

A final reminder: the best refinishers are old smoothies!

12. WOOD STAINS

Between the paint remover and the new finish to be applied come wood stains, both in importance and in job sequence. Wood stains are colorers that will make wood glow with brownish, reddish, yellowish, or other hues you may desire; they may be dark, light, medium, or any tone you wish. Staining is not hard labor, but the wrong approach has caused trouble at times. Stains are easy to use and easy to apply on all kinds of wood, provided you know what you are working with, and what they can and cannot do.

Hardware and paint shops have shelves filled with little cans of oil stains for wood, sitting there proudly under fancy names such as platinum, limed oak, provincial, fruit wood, modern wheat, old Salem, maple, straw, driftwood, butternut, softer pine, sage, blond, sun stroke, Mission, cherry, early Colonial, and many, many other products of the vivid imagination of advertising directors. But they are all basically ordinary stains with extraordinary names.

The shop will provide a color chart as your guide to choosing, but you will probably make a desperate choice in the end, or think you have made one when you see the results. Color charts are supposed to match the color of the stain in the cans—granted the manufacturer has tried to match them and to provide some kind of help—but these artificial wood tones will depend entirely on the kind of wood you apply them on, whether the wood is old and being refinished or raw new wood, and the amount of stain you apply to the wood.

The early Colonial mahogany may be one shade applied

to a certain species of wood and a completely different hue on another wood. The different woods accept the stains in their own peculiar ways, and if the wood has been impregnated or wood filler previously used, there is certainly a chance that you will get a different effect.

When applying stains, consider this. The solids of the pigment have invariably settled to the bottom of the can while it was resting on the shelf. Shake the can well to dissolve them and put them in solution again to get full value of your coloring. Heavy pigmentation, while fine for covering up blemishes or masking a bad piece of wood, will cover up and obscure beautiful natural wood graining. Professional refinishers do not use heavy solids in pigmenting their stains; they use mostly liquid clear tones, but they have their own sources of supply that are not wide-open to us, so we must make adjustments. The answer is to make a test before you go ahead with the whole thing. Try out the stain on some inconspicuous part of the article you are refinishing. The "wheat" stain you selected may turn into "delta mud" on your wood; the tone called "Ipswich" may more closely resemble "Mexico" on your finished product. Try them before you use them wholesale; if the first try is unsatisfactory, see what other shade or tone might give a result closer to the one you pictured. It is better to buy a new can than to live with a piece which will always irk you because it is not right.

Oil stains flow evenly and dry slowly which is why we prefer them to water- or alcohol-base stains. These latter are better stains for clarity and uniformity, but they penetrate so rapidly and dry so quickly that you will be in deep trouble if you have to overlap or do so by chance. The professional refinisher or the furniture manufacturer uses these stains in a sprayer and they suit his purpose better than they do ours.

Oil stains dry in slowly, and only moderate skill is required to use them perfectly well. Experts, manufacturers of stains, and even chemists may find something wrong with our method, but we can mix many shades of stain to our own satisfaction and the pigmentation will not cover up attractive wood graining. If all the wood grain is to be covered, the piece might as well be painted.

Our mixtures will dry more quickly than the full-bodied oil stains but for our purpose that is good. We can seal the stain and begin to finish all the sooner. In my small home workshop I have spent many long hours testing and trying in order to develop a common-sense method that avoids the usual disappointments. The stains are oily enough so that the first wiping on of stain *does not* sink in and dry, making it impossible to overlap the next stroke, if need be. The procedure is as follows.

Mix some of the basic stain colors to achieve the results you wish. Most of the stain colors for woods are basically brown, red, or yellow, in some tone or shade of the parent hue. They can be mixed to any shade you wish. Look at the color chart of the oil stain you have chosen and select the strongest tone of each of the following colors: dark brown, light brown, yellow, dark red, black. Many of them will have fancy names—but do not be confused; look at the *color*.

Your measuring device can be any small spoon, but keep it wiped clean from each dipping. The mixing vessel can be a plastic-coated paper cup. Here are some ideas of how to mix to achieve the color you desire:

TO GET	MIX TOGETHER
darker browns	basic dark brown with a drop or two of black
light brown	dark brown with light brown, half and half
dark reds	4 parts dark brown to 1 part dark red
light reds	3 parts light brown to 1 part dark red

dark golden tones	yellow and dark brown, half and half
light golden tones	4 parts yellow to 1 part dark brown
soft yellow tones	10 parts yellow to 1 part brown, light or dark

To apply, and to dilute to the strength of color or tone desired, mix the stain with mineral spirits (paint thinner). I usually mix half and half—1 part stain to 1 part thinner. You will have to experiment a bit to get the degree of lightness or darkness you wish, but the above recipes will give you a start toward the mixing of colors in the stains you may desire. Should you want to go into the fancier shades— honey maple or pumpkin pine brown, for instance—you will need a small tube of oil color in ultramarine blue. It is very strong, so use it sparingly to tone the browns, light or dark, to the shade you prefer. A tiny bit will go a long way in toning.

Mixing Your Own Stains

If you want to mix your own colors from scratch, you can get a wide assortment of shades by using the kind of oil paint artists use—"colors-in-oil" is the trade designation. They come in tubes of various sizes and vary in price according to the pigment. Possible choices are as follows, with approximate color description:

Burnt Umber	dark brown
Burnt Sienna	dark red-brown
Raw Sienna	yellowish
Vandyke Brown	grayish brown
Rose Pink	red
Ultramarine Blue	strong blue
Black	black

Always mix the oils with the pigment in the tubes before taking off the caps by squeezing the pigment back and forth in the tubes lightly—do not squeeze heavily or you will force the color out of the back end of the tube. This will again put the solids in solution with any oil that may have accumulated in the top of the tube, keeping the proportion of solid to oil in proper ratio.

When you make up your stain shade, you may follow the previously given formulas, mixing approximate quantities together. Or you may use the chart below. Dilute the pigment half-and-half with mineral spirits and try it out on some wood. If it is too light, mix more pigment and add it. If it is too dark, dilute with mineral spirits. A paper cup will again be your mixing vessel. The quantity will depend on the size of the area to be stained.

WOOD COLOR	PIGMENT COLOR
Dark walnut	Vandyke Brown
Light walnut	1 part Burnt Umber, 1 part Vandyke Brown
Dark cherry or maple	Burnt Sienna
Light cherry or maple	1 part Burnt Sienna, 1 part Rose Pink
Red mahogany	3 parts Burnt Sienna, 1 part Rose Pink
Dark oak	2 parts Raw Sienna, 1 part Burnt Sienna, 1 part Burnt Umber
Brown mahogany	3 parts Vandyke Brown, 1 part Rose Pink
Pine	3 parts Raw Sienna, 1 part Ultramarine Blue
Golden tones	2 parts Raw Sienna, 1 part Burnt Umber

The formulas above are, of course, only starting points for the amateur who will want to develop other stains to achieve other effects—honey, fruitwood, antique pine, or whatever color, shade, tone, or effect he wishes. Keep a record of colors used and proportions developed, so that if you want to duplicate a particularly good stain later on you can do it without guesswork and experimentation.

The stains used on antique furniture, where records are available, are not much help to the modern refinisher. Witness this old formula for a rosewood stain: alcohol, camwood, logwood, and aquafortis. Try to mix that one, let alone use it! If you wanted a yellow stain in the eighteenth century, in the time of Mr. Hepplewhite and Mr. Chippendale, you would have used lead, Paris white, bichromate of potash in various proportions. If it had to be a bluish color, you would have used copperas and prussiate of potash—if you could have found them. If the stain had to be brownish, you would have switched the copperas for sulphate of copper, providing you traded at a good store which knew what you required. Similar formulas were probably used in Early American furniture staining, for the books about furniture-making circulated and apprentices emigrated with the formulas in their clever little heads.

These formulas are long since outmoded, quaint and delightful as they sound. Today's craftsmen are more interested in a good result than in following quaint recipes, however authentic they may be.

13. THE STAINING PROCESS

Staining the wood does not mean putting blemishes in it but rather coloring the wood to give it a color other than its natural hue, to bring out the grain and to enhance the wood in other ways. Some woods in their raw state need stains to give them character since they have little of their own, and when woods such as gumwoods, beech, poplar, pine, maple, and birch (all of them light or colorless in the natural state) are used with veneers of other woods of character, they must be stained to tie in with them. Some woods may be finished in their natural state with no stain but the use of a stain will give them more character and make them livelier than they would normally be. Other woods—mahogany is one—are thought to be enhanced by the use of a colored stain. Mahogany finished in its normal state is brownish in color but the mahogany stain imparts a reddish cast to it which is very pleasant and, according to tradition, "right." Walnut is always brown, and there are also accepted colors for maple, birch, cherry, pine, and oak, sometimes more than one hue. This makes them the colors that are traditionally right for the woods.

Stripping furniture will usually remove most of the stain color that was applied originally. Often in furniture reproduced in later years a stain was applied to give it the tone that age alone would usually impart. Pine that has aged for two hundred years turns a beautiful mellow tone, but the clever refinisher can give a new piece of pine something of the same color. Formerly, craftsmen had to mix their own stains so it is impossible to state exactly what they used. In any case, today there are so many good stains available in such a wide array that you can probably find exactly the tone and shade you want by doing a little research in your paint dealer's shop.

Before you apply the stain, give the surface a good rubbing down with steel wool pads, using either #000 or #00, to make the surface as clean and as smooth as you can get it. Always rub *with* the grain, not *across* it. Rubbing across the grain will put tiny scratches across the wood which will show up badly in the final finish coats. Use rubber gloves when applying stains.

There are two or three kinds of stains—designated according to their base and use—but this section shall concentrate only on the oil stain* because it is the most satisfactory for our purpose. This will be applied with a lint-free cloth. (Only a small pad of folded cloth will be needed for wiping on the stain.) Be sure that you have the wood properly sanded and smoothed; this is the last chance you will have to do it and improperly smoothed places will take the stain unevenly. Try out the stain first to be sure it gives the proper tone you want. Either try it on an inconspicuous part of the piece or a similar piece of wood. Remember that when it is finished with the clear coating it will appear slightly darker than the hue you now see. Let it dry in well after you rub on the stain. You can thin the stain at this point with the solvent recommended on the can. Some refinishers prefer to do two stain coats, building up to a darker finish, and this may be done.

Cover the wood completely, doing one section at a time so that you can pick up excess stain quickly with the pad and

---

* Water- and alcohol-solvent stains penetrate and dry so quickly that if you overlap a previous coat you are in deep trouble; they will be doubly dark on the overlaps. That is why I advise oil stains for refinishing.

make it even. If you want it lighter, you can rub it with a clean cloth to pick up some of the stain. If it is too light, you can apply another coat of stain. If it is too dark when it begins to dry, you can moisten a clean pad with thinner and rub it again, lifting some of the excess stain and lightening it. You can work either way, to lighten or darken, for oil stains will not set or dry immediately.

Sealing Before Staining

If you have stripped an open-pored wood, such as mahogany, or a soft wood, such as pine or whitewood, too much stain can be absorbed readily without the prior treatment of a light or thin sealer. This rule also applies when you are going to stain new mahogany or soft woods like pine. Make your own sealer (see page 107) by mixing one-third white shellac and two-thirds alcohol. A little goes a long way. We generally mix in an old drinking glass and figure that a half glassful will do a good-sized table, at least.

Brush on quickly and easily—one coating. It will sink right into the wood and dry in about fifteen minutes. Then smooth the wood with a good rubdown with #000 or #00 steel wool to cut off any raised grain, and then stain. The results will be a much smoother and even staining. In almost all cases we follow this rule, whether we are working on soft or hard woods. Heavy and dense coatings of stain cover up attractive wood graining and do not enhance good finishing work.

If the oil stains were thinned down considerably with paint thinner, the stain should be dry enough in three or four hours, so you can proceed to seal the stain with another coating of the thinned-down shellac (one-third shellac and two-thirds alcohol).

If a full-bodied oil stain was applied, it may have to be given about twelve hours drying time before sealing.

Sealing in the Stain

This process is necessary to make certain that none of the stain applied to the wood will pick up in the brush when you are applying the finish coat and keep the stain from being the glass-clear coat it should be. Also, sealing tends to fill up the tiny pores in the wood so that the finishing coat can go on more smoothly and fewer finish coats will be necessary. Sealing is very easy to do, you can make your own sealer mixture.

White or colorless shellac and alcohol are mixed together. *Do not use wood alcohol or methyl alcohol.* Instead, purchase regular denatured alcohol, which is widely available at paint and hardware stores. Also, purchase small quantities of shellac at a time, as very old shellac has a tendency to stay tacky and not dry well. A little of this sealing mixture goes a long way. A glass container can be used for the mixing—an old drinking glass is ideal for this—and you can make your proportions as follows: Use a mixture of one-third shellac and two-thirds alcohol, but if the proportions vary a little one way or the other it does not matter too much. A quantity of about two-thirds of a glassful will give enough sealer for a moderate-sized table or two average chairs.

Stir the mixture well. Use a clean paint brush of the flat type about three inches wide. Brush on the sealer rapidly but take care not to slop it on. Avoid too much overlapping. The sealer will dry quickly and should be sufficiently dry to work on within a half hour or so. Feel the surface all over to make sure it is dry before attempting to smooth with steel wool again, and before applying the finish coats. From here on, all smoothing rubdowns should be with fine steel wool (#000 or #00). Make the rubdowns brisk, even, and without heavy pressure; the final coat's smoothness will depend upon the smoothness you create as you build.

Although there has been much clamor and much cautioning in books and articles about washdowns "raising the grain," I have never found any such trouble from using water. Nor have I ever found any rust from using steel wool, another bugaboo raised by some writers. If a piece is properly smoothed each time, as directed, and the piece carefully wiped off and dusted after each smoothing process, I guarantee no trouble will be encountered.

To make certain of this, use a tack rag—not the kind you pay money for at the shops, but one you make for yourself. These rags are used to pick up loose particles of dust and wood, so that the surface to be finished is completely dust free. Merely clean with a lightly dampened cloth and then allow ten minutes or so before applying another coating. To make a tack rag, moisten a piece of cheesecloth with water—a piece about the size of a face towel will do—and then wring it as dry as you can. Make it into a wad and pour a few tablespoonfuls of turpentine over it, working the cloth until it has penetrated to all parts. Wring it dry again, wad up the cloth once more, and then pour about two or three tablespoonfuls of varnish over it and thoroughly work it into the cloth, so that when the cloth is unfolded it has a uniform yellowish color. If it does not, put on a little more varnish and work it in again. The cloth should be allowed to dry a little before it is used; it should be barely damp and "tacky," hence the name "tack cloth." It should always be slightly damp so that it will pick up the dust and wood particles as it is used. Should it dry out in use, add small amounts of water and occasionally a little turpentine to keep it moist. Use the cloth folded to a size easy to use in the hand, and wipe the surface with it, turning it from time to time to offer a fresh pick-up surface. Between uses, keep the tack rag in a *tightly* closed jar or can with a screw-on cap, and always test it before using, to make sure it is properly "tacky."

NOTE: Some people prefer to use the turpentine and varnish together in a solution, thus saving the time and effort of two workings-in on the cloth. Fine. The main thing is to saturate the cloth and then wring out as much as possible of the turpentine and varnish, letting it dry until it becomes tacky and barely moist.

14. CHOOSING THE FINISH

A Personal Preference

There are so many finishes offered to-day and such alluring promises in the advertising for them, that it is almost impossible for the amateur to make a rational choice. Some of the newer finishes offer fast drying, or they are easier to apply; and, as always before, they mention toughness, durability, and flexibility. When it comes to penetration, we want true penetration, so that the coating sticks to the surface and stays there. It is not possible, even if it were the purpose of this book, to separate the good from the bad, or to mention trade names, or even all of the generic names. I can only present my own experience of refinishing and experimenting over the many years I have worked on furniture, refinishing it and enjoying all the things I have learned through the years.

Principally there are but two parts to a good finish on furniture: the liquid vehicle which evaporates and dries, and the solids which remain on the surface. Popularly named finishes usually employ one of these in the name—tung oil, phenolic, alkyd, urethane, and vinyl. There are many other resins, of course; take vinyl, for instance. It gets into the act in many furniture resins and house paints, and also gets into glue, tile flooring, fabrics, moisture-retaining wraps for food—and who knows what else? But this is not helping you to decide what kind of finish is best for the purpose you are contemplating.

I definitely prefer quality furniture varnishes for that is

our most dependable finish and it is traditional so that it is associated with antiques of many kinds. But there are other clear finishes of merit, such as penetrating sealers which contain vinyl or one or another of the synthetic resins. When you are putting on some of the synthetics you are laying a sheet of plastic not unlike the plastic sheets that package our groceries, our new clothing, and practically everything else nowadays. Remember this. If there is a deep scratch later on, it might occasion a complete "liftoff." I shall never be able to forget my own dismay in this regard. I had done a fine finishing job with one of the synthetics in the urethane class on a good old walnut desk. The preliminaries had been properly taken care of—finish removed, and everything well prepared. The finish coat flowed on beautifully with no odors; it dried beautifully and everything was splendid for a few days after the desk was put into use. Then something hit the edge of the desk—some small sharp instrument, apparently—and "liftoff" began. I thought I was witnessing the invention of plastic sheet manufacture! The desk had to be done over completely and I went back to the tacky, slower-drying varnish. I haven't yet found any reason to give it up.

What Kind of Varnish?

I have made hundreds and hundreds of tests and I have honestly tried to give every type of finish an even chance. Lacquer I do not like: It is not for home use because it is brittle, it will chip and craze, and it is toxic so that it must be used in a very well-ventilated place. It is also more explosive than other finishes. I leave it to the professionals with their spray equipment; I feel varnish is a better finish on all counts. A good varnish especially made for finishing furniture—or even a floor varnish—gives a clear resilient finish. But the emphasis here should be on good quality varnish.

How about penetrating sealers? Some teachers of furniture refinishing recommend a tung oil penetrating sealer. Well, it is a free society we live in and anyone can recommend anything, say or do anything he wishes. Therefore I shall just say that I prefer varnish because the plain common-sense approach works better for me with it. Penetrating sealers are excellent—on certain occasions. I am sure that the urethanes and vinyls have merits, too, but not for general furniture finishing by an experienced refinisher. You can brush, roll, or wipe them on, but the approved method on furniture is to wipe them on with "hand massage." You must be prepared for some disappointments if you use penetrating sealers on old furniture that has been stripped of previous finishes. The sealers may not penetrate and absorb as well as they should. On new wood, unfinished wood, they are very good, particularly on soft woods such as pine. They can penetrate and form a hard surface, drying quickly; in general they are not dangerous except for some which may contain nitrocellulose or a close relative of it. That must be used with good ventilation and away from sparks or fire.

They dry in quickly, these penetrating sealers, on new wood, but many of them dry from the top downward—not like our favorite varnishes which dry outward from the surface of the wood upward. Thus proper bonding when using sealers can be only a guess. The top surface may *feel* dry, but may not be dry below. You may be putting on a coat of wax (the kind that contains a petroleum distillate), and before your eyes and under your polishing rag the finish will start to go—and you will have a lot of fixing to do. Because of this quality, if you ever use such a sealer you should *apply no more than two coatings*.

Varnish, on the other hand, is tougher than shellac or even lacquer, and sturdy enough for any use you may select for it.

Most likely it will live in peace and harmony with you for the rest of your life. Penetrating sealers may be good on floors and on new wood, but they can be very touchy, very temperamental, when they are teamed with other chemicals in fillers, sealers, and stains from past eras, and with polishes of this era.

What about shellac, once the most popular furniture finish? It will make a fine and excellent-looking finish quicker than any other, but shellac may also be the source of much trouble. Water marks it and quickly ruins it, while alcohol is the solvent for shellac, so that it will completely ruin any wood finished with shellac. I use it only for sealing stains on wood, when refinishing, and for filling wood pores, in a greatly thinned solution, and that is the extent of it. It is not durable for table tops or any other place that will get wear or punishment, and that is a good enough reason to avoid it.

Another kind of wipe-on finish is called "Danish" or "Danish Modern." Although this is good, you do not need to purchase it—you can make your own wipe-on finish (see page 100). See the section on Wood Stains (p. 98) for the formula and the full method. Such a wipe-on finish requires many coats—two to three as a minimum—because such a thinned-down finish will give a very slow surface buildup. A quick job can be done on new wood—especially a nonabsorbent close-grained wood like maple. Allow time for thorough drying between coats, and smooth very lightly with fine steel wool or crocus cloth or the finest sanding paper before massaging on another coat.

The Only Varnish to Buy

When you have looked over all the kinds of varnishes offered—marine, spar, trim, one-hour, two-hour, four-hour, six-hour, dammar, elastic, bartop, rubbing, antique, or what have you—you will probably come back to one thing: varnish that can be thinned with turpentine or mineral spirits, and varnish that is *guaranteed to stand up against water, heat, and alcohol.* Spar varnish is excellent, but for *exterior* work. Such varnishes as are recommended here come in gloss, semi-gloss, satin, eggshell, low-sheen, or dull finishes. Many reputable manufacturers offer these products as you will learn when you visit your paint shop and make your selection. It is the final appearance of the piece and its durability which will be the test—not how you did it, but how it performs—although doing it right will help to insure a good performance and an enduring, good-looking finish.

15. FINISHING COATS

My favorite finish (see page 110) for furniture is varnish—and it has been a good finish used on fine furniture for a long time. Today we have a great many brands with almost as many formulas to choose from and we no longer must make up and mix our own, as was the case with earlier furniture makers and finishers.

I prefer a clear-finish coat that is a top-quality varnish containing tung oil or china wood oil, or one of the tough and durable resins called "alkyd," "phenolic," or "soya." You will find these names listed in the formulas on the labels of varnishes found at any reliable paint store. I prefer the semi-gloss or satin finish, but some people like the glossy coats. Varnish goes a long way so that usually only a small can need be bought; if you are not refinishing a great deal of furniture at a time, this will suffice. Never shake a varnish can vigorously or you will create air bubbles which may show up in the coating and cause trouble. Instead, stir the varnish slowly and carefully and you will come out better in the end. Mix small quantities of varnish at a time with 20 per cent to 25 per cent of volume of a paint thinner—mineral spirits is the proper name. Thin coats, built up on a surface, are better and more durable than a single thick coating and will be more easily applied, as well. A good varnish is fully guaranteed to stand up against hot water, alcohol, and white rings. The label will be your guide here, too.

A most important factor in putting on a good coating is the brush you use. It must be absolutely clean, flexible, and of the flat type. A two-inch or three-inch wide brush is best to use and a good one, properly cared for, can give good service for years.

Proper Care of the Brush

Some people are so unsure of having a clean brush that they buy a new one each time they do some refinishing. Others suggest that cleaning the brush with turpentine and then rinsing it several times in soap and water is sufficient before drying it. Everyone agrees that it is best to keep varnishing brushes only for use in varnishing, not for painting with other paints.

I follow a less expensive way than buying a new brush each time and a less troublesome one than washing them as outlined above, yet I always have clean finish brushes, new or old. As a matter of fact, my preference is for a well-broken-in brush. Here is how I keep mine clean: Use small, plastic-coated paper cups containing about a half-inch of lacquer thinner to wash varnish brushes. Swish it about well, washing out the varnish, then dispose of the thinner, pour in a fresh half-inch of it, and wash and clean the brush a second time. A third washing in another half-inch of lacquer thinner finishes the job. Now shake the brush out until it is almost dry and hang it up. This method is good for all brushes except the shellac brushes which must be washed out in a similar manner in alcohol, which is the solvent. The cost is very slight and each washing probably costs no more than a couple of cents.

Easy Way to Varnish

Even today there seems to be a "scare program" about varnishing. The proper way has been made to seem so difficult that it would appear that at least four years of apprenticeship was needed to learn all the technicalities about spreading varnish properly. I apparently never learned to recognize the "good" way from the "bad" way, because my naturally simple and easy technique has always worked and I defy anyone to find imperfections in it. I do not use the principle of making long perfect sweeps of the brush and tipping it, as is sometimes advocated. Maybe it is my habit of applying thinner coats that saves me every time. Here is how I varnish.

The first coat is applied for the purpose of putting a thin and uniform coating over the entire surface, regardless of whether you brush from the left, from the right, or forward and back. After the top has been covered with the least possible excess, then re-brush with more care and a little more pressure on the brush, using long sweeps *with* the grain of the wood across the entire surface. At the edge of the surface as you finish the sweeping stroke, you will find that the brush has picked up some excess varnish. Draw the brush across the edge of the varnish can or container to get rid of this excess and do it after every sweep on the brush. Try to work in a warm room with the varnish at room temperature. If the room is close to 70 degrees F. *and the varnish is similarly warm,* the varnish will level itself out after your final sweeps have completed the surface; when the varnish dries, you should have a nice smooth-finish coat. You will soon work into a smooth gentle flowing motion for the strokes and learn to gauge the pressure for these final strokes.

The number of coats is up to you. It all depends on what kind of surface you desire. For normal wear on table tops and tops of desks and dressers I suggest two or three coats. One coating on a close-grained wood such as maple may suffice—you must be the judge. I have a table that was given two coats thirty years ago and it has been in full use ever since, without ever looking shabby or needing refinishing.

If you want a "plate glass" finish, then you may have to use as many as five applications of glossy varnish.

Techniques for Coating Furniture

There is a definite technique to be worked out in applying varnish to furniture so that each surface is coated and covered properly. Let us take a table for our example. If we are going to varnish the entire piece, then handling becomes important as part of the technique. Put a generous padding of newspapers on the floor with plenty of them surrounding the outside edges so that no drips or drops will fall on the floor. Lay the table on this pad upside down. Varnish the underside of the top where it overlaps the apron or legs, leaving a hand hold on each side unvarnished if you wish, or varnish it all and touch it up later, after you have lifted the table up. Remember to do the work in as dust-free an atmosphere as possible and to wipe down the piece with the tack rag to remove accumulated dust and wood particles.

After doing the underside of the top, varnish the legs, using a brush lightly dipped so as to prevent runs and accumulations of varnish in the turnings or on the sides. Brush it a second time with the dry-brush technique just detailed to remove any excess. Then turn the table right side up (touching up the hand holds or the areas of varnish you have marred with fingermarks once it is set up). Now is the time to work on the top, and this is the part most frequently seen so that you must make it as fine as possible. When you have finished and carefully brushed the edges of the top to cover them and also to remove any excess that may form as drops on the underedge, leave the table undisturbed for at least twenty-four hours to dry in a minimum temperature of 65 degrees F. Stay away from it—and be sure that everyone else stays away—so that no dust is disturbed to fall on the drying surface. After the drying time, make a test in one or two inconspicuous places with your thumb or finger. If there are no thumbprints and no stickiness, make ready to apply the final coat of varnish—if you are doing only two coats—or the second coat if you plan more than two. Buff the surface lightly with #000 steel wool between each layer of varnish, then pick up any dust or steel particles left with a soft cloth that is only slightly damp, and allow ten minutes for the surface to dry before applying the next coat.

The varnish brush should be cleaned, of course, between coats and dried out in the drying period. Note the method advocated above for cleaning with lacquer thinner.

Shellacking for Final Coating

Shellac must be used somewhat differently. For one thing, it must be used only for pieces that will never be in contact with water or beverages—hence it is not used for table tops. Nor must it be used for surfaces that are likely to get hard wear. A picture frame, for instance, can be finished with shellac; furthermore, it can be back on the wall in two to three hours. Shellac is long wearing, but it is a more brittle coating than varnish and quite susceptible to discoloration or destruction from contact with moisture.

The shellac coat must be thin in order to cover well. The thinning formula should be different from that recommended for sealing, where mere coverage is desired. For finish coats we suggest that shellac be thinned half-and-half with *denatured* alcohol. (Please note that this is *not* wood alcohol or methyl alcohol.) Denatured alcohol is available at paint and hardware stores. Mix the white or colorless shellac and alcohol in a glass container. An old drinking glass is ideal unless a greater quantity is needed. Fill the glass receptacle a little less than half full of shellac, then fill the glass with about an equal quantity of alcohol, leaving a little space at the top for stirring without slopping over. Stir and mix thoroughly. As you work, if the shellac gets a bit thick from evaporation, add a small quantity of alcohol and thin it again.

Shellac in alcohol sets quickly because of the fast evaporation of the alcohol so the coating must be brushed on thinly and quickly, keeping the brush strokes in one direction as far as possible. Overlapping of strokes will not matter too much if the shellac is still wet—the fresh shellac will tend to put the old stroke back into solution—but remember to brush on *thinly* to avoid buildups that may show. Pick up excesses as you go along, and when the coating is finished allow it to dry for an hour or so. Usually it will be dry in less than an hour, although not yet "cured." Lightly rub it with #000 fine steel wool and then dust it off with a dry cloth. Spread a second coat of shellac and again allow it to dry for an hour. After that, as soon as it is polished, the piece is again ready for use.

Professional refinishers usually use more in-between rubdowns than the quicker and easier steel-wool rubdowns outlined here, to be sure that the surface is smooth and right. You may also encounter some difficulty with certain pieces; if the surface has not been thoroughly smoothed before the first coat of shellac, and rough spots show up after the finish has dried, you may have to take extra care before going on. If the steel-wool rubdown does not completely smooth such spots, give the piece a second rubdown with a very fine silicone carbide sanding paper; for curved surfaces and legs or rungs, use a very fine emery cloth. Work with a gentle and even pressure, using the sanding paper on a small wooden block for flat surfaces, so that you can control it. Do not press too hard or work too long, for such abrasives cut quickly. Some refinishers advocate using a rubdown of very fine pumice abrasive mixed with oil and applied with a thick piece of felt. I used to use this method but decided I was putting too much effort into the operation without sufficient gain in results, so I have not used it since. Nor have I missed it.

Other Finishes for Furniture

So far I have detailed my choices of the best, most durable, and easiest furniture finishes. There are other good finishes, too.

One wipe-on finish is composed of 50 per cent varnish (any of those specified previously), 30 per cent turpentine, and 20 per cent boiled linseed oil. If you choose a varnish with a tung-oil base, then you have for all practical purposes the same finish used on Danish modern furniture, and packaged for sale under the name of Danish Modern Finish. A similar finish is a tung-oil penetrating sealer wipe-on finish, which is sold under brand names in paint stores.

In all wipe-on finishes the process is the same. Be sure that the wood is thoroughly prepared and smoothed. Use a lint-free cloth (cheesecloth is good) and fold it into a pad of several thicknesses. Saturate the pad with the finish and wipe it on, massaging it in with the cloth, or your hands, to apply as much finish as possible at a time on each coat. When you have covered the entire area, wipe off the excess oils and allow to dry for about a week before applying the next wipe-on coat to the surface. Between coats rub down with steel wool (#000 grade) or with very fine silicone carbide paper. Apply a coat each week until you have built up as much finish as you judge you will need.

The boiled linseed-oil finish, which is an old-fashioned method, I do not particularly like. The surfaces become sticky and gummy, especially during hot humid weather, and for this reason I cannot advocate its use on chairs. The method is the same—wiping on the oil, rubbing and rubbing, removing the excesses, and allowing the oil to dry-in between coats. The classic method is once a day for a week, once a week for a month, once a month for a year, and then once a year for the rest of your life. This is too arduous, even though the final finish is not hurt by water, cannot be scratched, or, if the surface should be abraded, it is easy to apply more oil and rub it in again to refinish a small part. I like hard, dry surfaces that stay dust-free and therefore recommend the other wipe-on finishes. See page 121.

Lacquer, despite a fine quality of transparency which allows the wood to show through beautifully, has far too many disadvantages for recommendation here. There are two types of lacquer—brush-on and spray. Spraying is out of the question; it entails purchase of equipment and the dangers in its use because of its explosive qualities put it outside the realm of home shops. The brush-on types are less dangerous to use, but require greater skill. They have less flexibility than varnish and may show craze marks after a bit of use.

Polishing After the Final Coat

In order to keep your finish in good shape and your furniture with the soft sheen that good wood deserves, polishing is necessary after finishing coats have been applied.

There are so many furniture polishes and their descriptions are so glowing (in the advertising, not always from users) that we cannot attempt to separate the good from the bad. The public wants a miracle polish—one that will apply itself, polish itself, and maintain itself in perfect condition for years—so manufacturers keep attempting to supply their version of this, subject always to their need to stay in business from constant resale of the product, of course. From the beginning of this wax-polish business, about 1898, until the present time we have seen many variations—no-rub shines, pressure sprays, emulsions, pastes, and odorous liquids—offered to those who want furniture to take care of itself. Some polishes look good for a day or two until too much dust accumulates on them. Some never look good from the very beginning. Some give the FBI competition in taking fingerprints. There was a time when a lemon-oil smell was popular until it was superseded by other odors; now it is on the upsurge again. A lemon *smell* gives no more assurance of a good polish than a raspberry or huckleberry smell does.

After trying all kinds of things and observing their failures, I have concluded that you cannot do better than to use a good quality of hard carnauba wax polish that comes in paste form. It will keep your furniture dry with its hard finish, giving a durable, fingerprintless sheen. Dust will not stick to it as it does to most other polishes. There may be a little extra work in the beginning, but as time goes on, there will be ever so much less work. A once-a-year polishing will keep the surfaces in good condition and this I find superior to pushing a spray can around every fifth day or so.

The softer beeswax polish is a favorite with some people. If you have one of these polishes that you like, stick with it. You might be doing worse (unless you switch to carnauba wax) if you try another.

Waxing Properly

Polishing is dependent upon applying the wax properly— provided you have followed earlier directions and now have a smooth surface on your final coat of refinishing materials. A good coating of wax on several coats of shellac will protect it well and help it to wear for a long time. Waxing will protect and enhance the dust-repelling qualities of varnish, too. Therefore, to have a really good wax job, it should be laid on properly, with all care given to it in the beginning. It will save work later on.

A word or two of caution: If your final finish was a penetrating sealer or had one of the other synthetics as an ingredient in its composition, a longer time should be allowed for it to dry thoroughly than is necessary for varnish made with tung oil or alkyd resin, for instance. Paste wax has mineral or petroleum spirits used in its composition and many of the new synthetics do not take kindly to these spirits until they have been thoroughly dried, or "cured." They may be dry to the touch, but they will not be cured for several days, so it will be wise to delay final polishing. A week is usually enough time to wait.

Carnauba is the hardest wax known for use in polishing. It comes from a tree that grows in Brazil and for more than a generation it has proved itself the best wax to use on furniture. Smear on a thin layer of the hard paste wax and let it dry thoroughly. Then buff it lightly with a clean pad of #00 or #000 steel wool—not a cloth. A cloth will, of course, pick up wax, but a steel wool pad will generate a little heat and keep the wax where you want it—it will be smoother than if a cloth was used. At the start, it is a little extra effort to make, but the total work will be far less, for this kind of finish will last and last, with no gummy buildup and no fingerprints. Remember—buff it *lightly!*

Stay strictly away from silicone polishes. They seem to get into everything and once they are in a refinishing shop you are headed for a heap of trouble. Silicones make wonderful slippery lubricants but they are the worst enemy to finishes that are drying out. Therefore, steer clear of them, and of cheap paraffin-oil or wax shines, as well.

The use of these "miracle" polishes on your already refinished furniture can give you trouble. With clean rags, remove all that sticky, gummy residue from the miracle polishes with paint thinner and then rebuild the finish with honest carnauba hard-paste wax. The colorless (white) or the colored (dark brown) both have their uses and both will give a dry sheen—the best protective polish I have yet found.

Polishing once or twice a year in the beginning will build up a good polish finish. After that, polish only when you feel the surfaces need brightening.

When the furniture polish industry develops an effortless, space-age product, I shall be most interested to try it and compare it with the fine polish that carnauba hard-paste wax gives to furniture. But not until then.

16. DECORATING WHILE REFINISHING

There are a number of processes or operations by which furniture can be enhanced in refinishing in order to gain certain effects or to cover up defects. Only the more popular and practical of them will be discussed here, in order to give adequate coverage to the safe and easy ways to achieve decorative results. There are several approaches and an understanding of what may be gained by them and how they are done will give you a good base from which to work. The only basic requirement is to be endowed with some furniture that needs something more than ordinary refinishing.

ANTIQUING. If the piece has been previously painted, rather than finished with a clear finish so that the wood shows through, or if it is in such bad condition that nothing but a paint job will suffice to make it presentable, then antiquing may be the very thing that will make the piece interesting and unusual. Oftentimes you can even do the painting right over the old finish, if it is not too deeply scarred. Or if there are scratches and scars, they may even add to the old look you are aiming for. So long as the old coats are firmly bonded to the wood, you can antique with confidence and hide most of the defects rapidly. New furniture, bought unfinished but of proper design and proportioned to go well with real antiques, may also be painted and antiqued. Or in the case of certain styles, such as French Provincial and certain of the country styles of American furniture, or on the interiors of cabinets and bookshelves, painting and antiquing is the proper and authentic period approach. Therefore this is one of the most important processes for the amateur refinisher.

First, clean the old surface so that there will be no grease or other materials such as wax or furniture polish which might interfere with proper bonding of the coats of paint you will be applying. Use mineral spirits or paint thinner on a soft cloth. Sand the paint or the wood lightly to smooth it and to remove surface glaze if it is painted, thus allowing the paint to bind itself when applied. Brush on the base coat of paint, brushing *with the grain.* (If the grain is not visible, brush the longest way on the surface being covered.) Make sure no grain imperfections or color from the undercoats show through. If necessary, apply a second coat of base paint. Allow it to dry thoroughly, at least overnight. For added safety, a day or two will make sure that there is no chance of its not being dry.

The second step is to apply the glaze color, usually a dull and subtle shade that will harmonize with the paint or contrast with it pleasantly, or it may just make the undercoat look more aged and used. The glaze coat is thin and it will be wiped off the piece but allowed to stay in certain places—the crevices of carving, the pores of wood, the turnings of legs or spindles, around hardware—in order to bring out and enhance these features and to make them look as if they had been in use for a long time with a buildup of natural darkening around them where dusting and washing down had not removed surface soil. Most glazes you buy will be Burnt Siennas and umber tones or the more brownish ochers. Or, if you buy an antiquing kit, the glaze comes all ready for use, color keyed to the base color you select. If you are more creative, you may want to make your own glaze. But be sure that the two kinds of paint you use are compatible—oil paint for applying on oil paint, latex paint for latex paint, and so on. Specific directions for application will be found in the photographic section (page 187). For mixing glazing paints, you may use your own oil colors if you have some left—and a small amount will generally suffice when thinned down. Color light colors with either artists' oil-painting colors or the tinting colors that are available in paint stores. For a quick reference, some of the oil colors which may be used are appended, with descriptions:

Burnt Umber	dark brown, neutral to yellowish-brown
Burnt Sienna	dark red-brown
Raw Sienna	light yellowish-to-brown
Vandyke Brown	grayish-brown
Rose Pink	reddish
Ultramarine Blue (ultra)	deep, dark blue

There are other ways in which a piece can be embellished and given an antique flavor. It depends entirely on the piece and what effect will be suitable and desirable, of course, what approach you will make.

If an old finish is sound but rather gloomy in appearance, it can be made more vigorous and exciting by touching up all the high spots with gold. Buy gold bronzing powder (available in small bottles at paint stores) in either light gold, antique gold, or whatever shade of gold will harmonize with your piece. Mix a small quantity of the bronzing powder with about an equal quantity of varnish, thinned slightly with turpentine. Brush on this mix wherever you want a touch of gold to shine through, and let it dry. When it is thoroughly dry, apply a coat of whatever color paint will harmonize with the piece you have—bone white, pale green, deep brown, red, or (on red- or orange-base color) black. After the coat is brushed on—do only one side or one area at a time to prevent too-quick drying of the antiquing coat—wipe off the high spots where you have applied the gold and wipe lightly over the other areas as for general antiquing. After all the paint has thoroughly dried, apply a protective glaze coating of thinned varnish over all.

A few additional tips may not be amiss. The paint used may be flat, semi-gloss, or high gloss, though in general a matte finish is to be preferred to high gloss lest the very newness and shininess of the appearance defeat the purpose of antiquing, that is, to make the piece look old and mellow. Such antiqued pieces can appropriately be placed in bedrooms, dining rooms, family rooms, and playrooms, while a piece or two in a living room may lend exactly the right touch to a corner that needs brightening.

Antiquing kits, mentioned earlier, are efficient and easy to use. The price is reasonable and the usual kit is composed of three cans of finish: one can is the base coat, the second is the contrasting color that is brushed on the base coat, and the third is the protective clear finish. The kits come in regular paint colors and also in wood tones such as mahogany, fruit wood, walnut, driftwood, teak, and so on. Wood-tone kits may contain a fourth can of glaze, together with complete directions on how to use these glazes to the best advantage. Basically the kits with their complete sets of finishes, sanding paper, brush for applying the finishes, and even cheesecloth for wiping off the glaze are like a complete workshop in one box. Their use is similar to what is outlined above. In addition to the oil-paint kits (which may require some time for complete drying between coats) there are also some kits that use latex paints, water thinned and quicker drying so that you might be able to finish the job in a single day.

To sum up what is required for antiquing, remember these common-sense procedures:

1. Clean old surfaces well with water and detergent or wash with a rag and mineral spirits to be sure no wax or grease or dirt will impede the work and the adherence of the paint.

2. Make sure the base coat is sound, repaint if necessary, and use fine sandpaper to give a proper "tooth" for the paint coat.

3. Apply the glaze coat—no need to be too careful, for the appearance of age is what is required. Do not attempt to cover too great an area at one time.

4. Wipe off the glaze, bearing heavily on projections and on areas in centers, but less heavily toward edges of panels and sides or edges of tops. Do not wipe out deep-cut carvings or low cuts in turnings and moldings. The highlights should have the least glaze left, shading down toward the deeper cuts so that it looks as if age and use had worn away the glaze.

5. Varnish the whole piece to protect the glaze and paint and to insure that it will be durable. A semi-gloss or flat varnish effect is usually more desirable than is a high gloss varnish unless there is a special reason to use a glossy one.

GRAINING.   Although graining predates antiquing as a form of fakery in furniture finishing, little is heard about it today. It once had the reputation of being very difficult and tricky, an art that few could do well, but actually it can be reduced to the definition of "a kind of beautiful smearing." It requires a little practice but can be mastered by most refinishers. It is particularly useful for covering up wild grains on wood, cheap and mean-looking woods, and there are many possible grains to achieve—curly maple, crotched walnut, satinwood, or mottled mahogany such as comes from the heart of Africa. Try it and fool yourself and everyone else who looks at the furniture.

Buy a wood-grain kit at the paint store to try out the method. Later on you may make up your own kit from the oil colors and varnish as suggested in the preceding pages on Antiquing. You will use the earth or wood colors in oil for this, of course.

The method is simple. Apply a light brownish varnish over the entire surface and let it dry. Then apply a coat of reddish varnish and, after it has set a little, wipe over this still-wet surface with a stiffish paint brush going in straight patterns or wavy, circular motions to simulate the grain of wood. Keep wiping the excess paint lifted off from the tips of the bristles; a dry brush to lift off the excess is the secret of the trick. Graining can also be done with a rumpled rough cloth or newspaper. It takes a bit of practice, but once you get the hang of it, observe woods and you'll be able to duplicate almost any natural grain, adapting it to your own design. Many a door still swings which was made from the cheapest wood but looks like a fine piece of wood because it was cleverly grained to look that way.

Graining with paints, using the same antiquing paints, is also very effective. You can practice on a picture frame that has an uninteresting molding. Put on a base coat of color, and when it is dry, try a second coat, making the graining swirl, wave, or circle about with the brush or cloth wiping. Or use a base coat of gold bronzing powder and varnish, then grain it in deep blue or red, or some other color. A base coat of bone white can be grained with light browns or a darker greenish-bronze color, or any color that suits the room. It is a fascinating and very interesting art to master.

PICKLING. This is a quick and easy process which is called by some "modern," but it is especially effective on old furniture with very porous wood, such as oak. If you are tired of a dirty, dreary golden oak table, strip off the finish, smooth it, then seal it with a sealing mixture of 30 per cent clear shellac to 70 per cent alcohol. Allow this to dry for a half hour, then brush on a heavy coat of flat white or bone white paint. Allow the paint to set for a short time, then wipe across the grain with a coarse rag, picking up all the paint except what adheres and remains in the pores. Be sure not to wipe the paint out of the pores, but leave them well filled. When this is dried—leave it for a day—apply one or two coats of your own thinned-down varnish (80 per cent varnish to 20 per cent thinner compatible with varnish, see label), allowing each coating to dry and then rubbing down with fine steel wool after the coating has dried. Polish the wood with a hard paste wax. The piece is now ready for use.

Other effects can be obtained by pickling; you can use tints of other colors—green, red, blue, or dark colors on light wood, too. If it is pickled, furniture with wooden frames, especially carved wood frames, can be made to go with the upholstery colors and to bring out the design without destroying the wood color, as would happen if it were painted. Mahogany takes on a fine grayish tone when pickled, oak of the darker-stained varieties shows its grain beautifully, and other woods of open grain also profit by being pickled.

BONING. This is actually antiquing, except that white paint is always used and Raw Umber is the color used for the glaze. Seal the wood and apply the paint, giving it a second coat if necessary to cover it well. Use the glaze coat and wipe it off to give it an aged, somewhat dirtied look. Then after it is dry, apply thinned varnish to give protection.

SPATTERING. ("Spatterdash," it is sometimes called.) Originally used mostly on floors, and still much used on the wide floor boarding of old houses when they are restored, the use of spatter can also be applied to furniture. The process is simple. Apply the base coat of paint as usual and allow the paint or enamel to dry thoroughly. Use a paint of similar makeup (oil base, for example) and of a different color. Often two to six different colors are used for spattering over the base coat. Use a stiff paint brush or a small whisk broom, a vegetable brush or, for very fine spatterwork, as on a box or small object, use a toothbrush. Dip the brush lightly into the paint, then flick it, causing it to make drops which will be larger or smaller, according to the tool used. The distance of the brush from the surface spattered will also be a factor. Some painters use a piece of wood to spring the bristles back and cause them to release the paint. Again, practice will show you how to do this effectively. Spattering can be used on the top of a table or desk, if the rest of the painted piece is kept covered with newspapers held in place by masking tape. Spatterwork is useful in making paint look like marble, for the spatters can be done irregularly and blurred slightly before marbleizing strokes for veins are applied. Also, spatters can give picture frames the look of age. A too-bright gilded frame which would shriek in an antique setting can be toned down a little with glaze and then a very light spattering of black be done to simulate age marks on the gold. After spattering, polish with a hard paste wax to protect it or, in the case of floors, give the entire surface a coat of a good, hard, clear, full-bodied varnish.

TRANSFERRING (Decalcomanias). These are used to decorate painted furniture or walls and numerous designs are available at various places—paint stores, department stores, and hardware shops. Few of the designs are appropriate for antiques, but if you can find ones you like, their use is easy. The transfers, or "decalcomanias" as they are also called, are colored, printed designs on a transparent film which slides off the paper backing when it is moistened. Soak the paper first, then slide the transfer off it and onto the painted surface you wish to decorate, positioning it carefully. Wipe the transfer carefully from the center to expel the moisture from under it and smooth out air bubbles so that it will dry flat and adhere uniformly. When it is perfectly dry, varnish it.

PAPERING, self-adhering type.   In hardware and paint stores, as well as in other places, will be found a wide variety of self-adhering papers that are plastic coated for durability. The designs are attractive and many can be used as backing for bookshelves or to paper the inside shelves of china cabinets. These are very easy to use; the backing is coated with a very powerful adhesive that sticks to the surface of the place to be coated and adheres on contact. The paper backing is peeled off, exposing the adhesive, then the paper is applied. Cut and shape to fit the area to be covered before removing the backing. Allow a slight overlap to cover any gaps that might occur at edges.

STENCILING.   This is important because of the extensive use made of it by Lambert Hitchcock, the Connecticut cabinetmaker who developed the famous Hitchcock chairs early in the nineteenth century. Stencils were used to decorate the backs of most of the Hitchcock chairs, gold on black being a favorite device with occasional departures in favor of other schemes.

While entire books have been devoted to stenciling and how to develop the amazing possibilities of this art, the approach here is kept simple for the beginning amateur. Once started, if you wish to pursue stenciling further, you can find many excellent books on the subject.

First, buy a piece of architects' tracing linen at an art

supply store. Though it is expensive by the yard you will not need much of it for your work, probably fifty cents worth. Measure the area in question and then buy enough to cover it—the minimum amount sold may suffice. Put the linen over the design you wish to follow or sketch it freehand on a paper and then trace with a soft pencil on the linen. Cut out the designs with cuticle or embroidery scissors. If the lines are straight, you will be able to use a sharp-pointed knife or a razor blade to cut it. Remember that you must leave some attachments here and there to hold the design together as you stencil, so plan in advance of cutting where you will place these for the greatest strength. They need be only one-eighth of an inch wide.

Next, prepare the furniture to be stenciled. The base coats should be applied and allowed to dry and the last layer of varnish should be drying before you attempt to stencil. This coat should be nearly dry but still tacky enough to hold the stencil in place. If the varnish feels like clear cellulose sticking tape, tacky but not wet, then it is about right, and it will receive and hold the bronzing powder you will use.

Lightly press the stencil in place, making sure it is flat all over. Make a piece of velvet into a one-finger glove and with this apply the bronze powder. Select the color of gold you wish to use and put some of it on a paper so that you can dip into it easily. You can apply the powder evenly all over the stencil or you can learn to fade it out quickly so that you get a shaded effect. The velvet fingertip makes it easy to control this application.

After dusting on the gold, remove the stencil carefully and gently and then clean the stencil on both sides with turpentine and allow it to dry out before using it again. A stencil can be used over and over, if carefully cleaned after each use. Apply a coat of clear varnish over the stenciled design after the gold has thoroughly dried into the varnish and any excess has been wiped carefully away. If it is on a hard-wear spot, give it two or three coats of varnish.

I have made crude stencils of heavy wrapping paper varnished on both sides and allowed to dry and I have used unorthodox methods of applying the bronzing powder. I have used just my fingertip with the dry powder and I have also used powder mixed with a minimum amount of varnish. I have used a fine sponge, too, as well as a stencil brush, a round, flat-ended bristle brush which is lightly tamped over the stencil to dislodge the bronzing powder, or gold powder mixed with varnish, or paint. You can try almost anything and if it works, you have a new technique to use.

Originate Your Own "Antiques"

It is possible to make up from various components some entirely new and useful pieces. For instance, if you happen to run across an old warped bowl made of wood, you might look for an old wooden tabouret or fern stand. Remove the flat top of the tabouret and glue and screw on the wooden bowl, making a receptacle for sewing, knitting, and other articles about the house. It can be painted and stenciled or it can be kept in natural wood, provided the woods of bowl and pedestal are not too dissimilar.

Antique sap buckets of metal or wooden firkins also make attractive accessories, and an old metal milk can with a neck and side handles can be painted and antiqued, stenciled or painted with posies or designs to make it fit your style of decoration. I found one in the town dump not long ago, probably dropped there by someone who knew I would be along that day. They wouldn't recognize it now. Paint can do a great deal to make an old piece of "junk" look interesting and give it a new lease on life. See pages 190, 194.

PART III

The Methods to Be Used

GETTING ACQUAINTED
WITH A LIQUID SOLVENT PAINT REMOVER

The top photograph shows how to *flow* on a good quality, heavy-bodied, nonflammable liquid paint remover, filling the brush from an old coffee can. The old board has about five coats of modern oil paints and this kind of remover will attack oil paints in seconds.

The center photograph shows the result of my first guess, that the paint remover would go through to the wood in about fifteen minutes, but it has not as you can see. I pushed off a section of the sludge and discovered that the remover had not yet gone through bottom darkish paints, so I applied another layer of paint remover and waited fifteen minutes more.

Now, see the grain of the wood in the bottom photograph—a typical softwood fir grain. This is the time to remove everything with the steel wool and washdown process, or by pushing and scraping, followed by a final cleanup with rags and paint thinner, if the water-wash method is not used.

COMMENTS. In the center photograph the remover application did not completely cover the front edge of the board, deliberately done to show better how paint remover wrinkles up oil paints. Note also that *you* have to do the removing and that liquid paint removers do not remove a thing. Note also that much of the power of the paint remover was lost for as the wrinkles raised so high the remover was lifted away, losing its effectiveness. This big wrinkle effect—this lifting—is dramatic, but costly. A liquid paint remover that has a tendency to "sink" through the old finishes without lifting or bubbling up is the better paint remover. Removers that sink through and stay wet for a long time are the most efficient. If it's drama you're looking for, go to the theater!

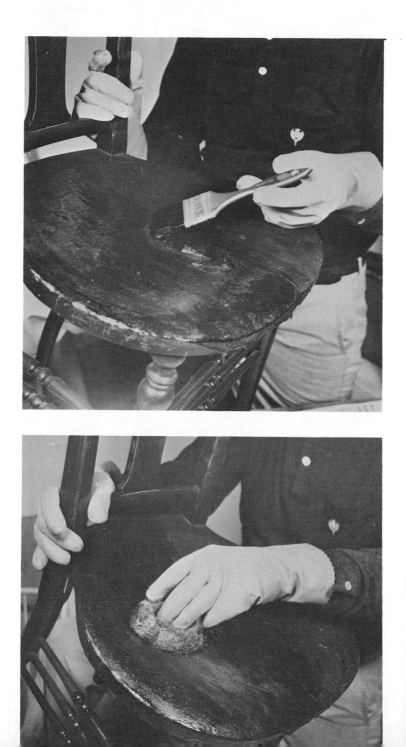

o ps

FINISH REMOVAL—FLAT SURFACES

Flat or nearly flat areas are best kept as horizontal as possible in order that a good thick coating of remover can be applied and left to do its work on the finishes. When large boxlike pieces of furniture are being refinished—desks, dressers, chests, bookcases, and the like—work on one surface at a time, turning the piece to a new side as each of the other sides is completed and finish removed.

METHOD. Wear rubber gloves and old clothes for this is a messy operation. A rubber apron or other additional protective covering may be helpful. Spread a thick padding of newspapers over the area before you set up the piece to be refinished to prevent unnoticed drips of remover from falling, soaking through and damaging a wood floor. Even on concrete a newspaper pad will facilitate cleanup after the job is finished. Use the remover in a container such as a coffee can so that the brush can be easily dipped and refilled. Take big brushfuls, or pour a moderate amount on the surface and spread thickly with the brush, leaving a liberal coating all over; avoid thin spots, and make the coating as even as possible. Do not rebrush once the coat is laid for this may hasten evaporation and lessen the effectiveness of the remover. In the top photograph opposite, note how, even before surface is completely covered, the finish is bubbling and loosening as solvents begin to work. Allow twenty to thirty minutes after application so that remover can cut through to lower coats. Test to see how far it has penetrated and if it has gone far enough, begin removal. Use a steel wool pad to scrub off loosened finish. If, when sludge is removed, there are still spots of old finish or if remover has not gone through all of the old finish coats, reapply remover, repeat operation until wood comes clean and finish has all been removed.

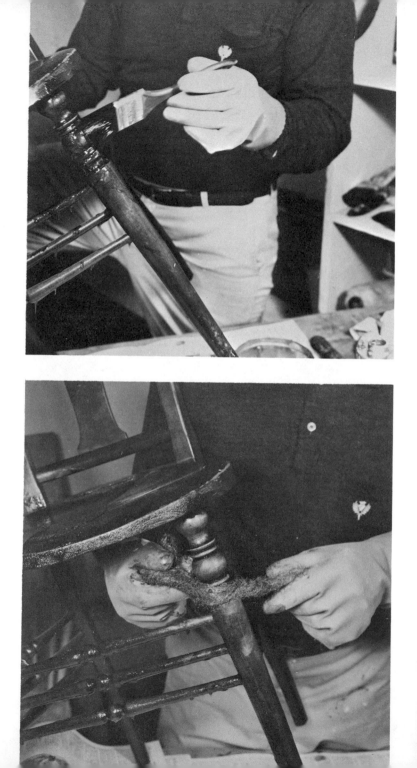

REMOVING FINISH FROM TURNINGS

It is sometimes difficult to take the finish off turnings that decorate legs, spindles, and rungs because the old finish is gummed up and lodged in the crevices. Nevertheless, all of the old finish must be removed or it will cause trouble and look bad under the new finish, and detract from the clean, sharp lines of the turned round piece. On rounds that have no turnings or decorations, the usual methods may be employed—apply paint remover, allow to sit until finish is loosened, use steel wool pads to remove sludge, and wash down to remove residue. But for turnings such as those seen on chair legs in the photograph opposite, a different method is effective. Apply a heavy coat of paint remover (top photograph) and while it is softening the finish, pull a steel wool pad into a longish "rope" (see bottom photograph). When paint is loosened, grasp each end in rubber-gloved hands, work it back and forth around the turnings, and pull it well down into crevices between turnings. Use a new piece of steel wool as often as the old one becomes loaded, or wash it out in the water-wash mixture. If necessary, reapply paint remover to loosen stubborn finishes or spots. Occasionally small spots may still remain and these may be carefully scraped with a dull knife-blade to make sure that all of the old finish is taken off so that the wood will be completely clean before the new finish is applied.

REMOVING FINISH FROM CARVED WORK

To remove softened finish from deep crevices in carvings, in fluted work, or in turnings on legs, a stiff-bristled brush is used. A soft wire brush may also be employed, but stiff wire brushes are likely to leave scratches which scar the wood and show up in the transparent final finishes. Brushes can be easily washed out to use again for future jobs.

If possible, always remove drawer pulls and other hardware, such as hinges that show on the outside of the piece, *before* removing the finish. If metal, they can be soaked in paint remover, cleaned, and then polished; if wood knobs and drawer pulls are the original equipment, they can be repainted or refinished with stain and clear varnish. After the piece has been completely refinished, replace drawer and other hardware where they belong.

METHOD. Apply the paint remover generously and let it sit for a time to do its work. Hold or place the piece in as horizontal a position as possible so that the remover will not run off it. Place the piece in a good light and keep turning it as you work to be sure that you see all of the spots and remove all of the paint or finish. Working on a low table or bench or even on a box enables you to see what you are doing. Use steel wool pads to remove as much of the finish as possible, then use the brush to get into the crevices and cracks to work the softened finish out. If the first application does not soften sufficiently to get all the finish off, repeat the process. Washing off water-soluble remover is the easiest way to get all finish off carvings and turnings.

WASHING OFF FINISH

The water-wash method is used; this means quick, easy, clean removal of sludge. If you have a yard where you can hose down the piece afterward, removal is practically painless. It will squirt off very easily with a hose nozzle adjusted to a thin, strong jet. One caution, though: do not wash the piece near a painted wall or fence—the splatters may get on the other paint. For those who must wash by hand, or prefer to, the method is almost as easy.

METHOD. Prepare a pail of water with a solution of a cupful of TSP and a half-cup of heavy-duty detergent to a pailful of warm water. Wear old clothes and heavy rubber gloves for the work, to protect against smears and spots and to protect the hands. Use a steel wool pad, dipping it frequently into the pail to clean out the sludge and to load it again with the solution. I often use the cement floor of my garage to wash down furniture (see photograph), hosing the residue out the door of the garage and washing it down the drain. Heavy pads of newspapers can also be used, facilitating the cleanup afterward. Always wash down with clear rinse water afterward and then wipe the piece dry with a clean, soft cloth. Allow it to dry out well before attempting to go on with the finishing process.

WHAT CAN THE NEW POWDER PAINT REMOVER DO?

Demonstrating the powers of a new paint remover, useful for taking off coats of heavy paints, particularly multiple coatings. The top paddle shows the effect of *one* application on a few coats of paint, brought down to raw wood on the board as seen in the clear patch down the middle. Below is another, but older, professional paint-mixing paddle. It holds at least a hundred thick coats of paint—it was never cleaned off after use in stirring—and it was brought down to the wood with several successive applications of powder paint remover and washings to remove the sludge. This powder paint remover is useful on antique paints, such as buttermilk and other homemade paints, doing the jobs that liquid paint removers cannot do efficiently, if at all.

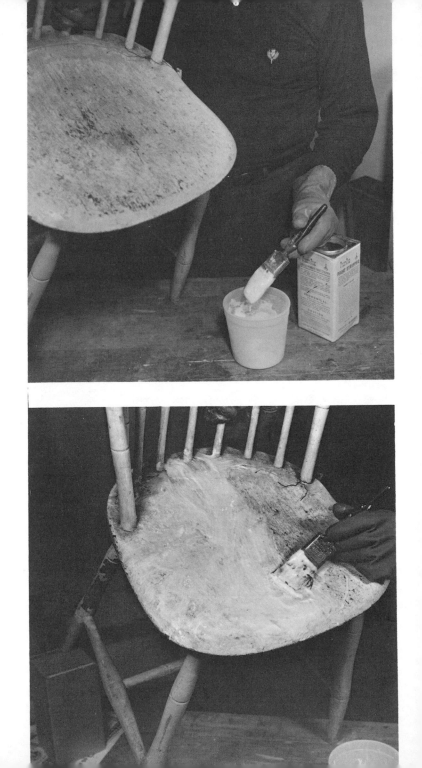

ANTIQUE PAINTS

Paints of various composition will be found covering antiques and many of them are difficult to remove. Modern removers may be annoying because they utilize solvents which work slowly and are not suited to removal of paints a hundred or more years old. One such is buttermilk paint which often resists and even defies the ministrations of the refinisher. Much hand scraping and consequent damaging to finishes or woods may be entailed with the average paint removers; perhaps, finally, the only answer is to sand off the finish—a laborious procedure. A new kind of paint remover (see page 71) works very well on such paints and strips them down to bare wood with a minimum of effort. Sludge washes off easily, too.

METHOD. Prepare remover mixture according to package directions. Remover comes as a dry powder to be mixed with water and must be allowed to sit for a short time before being ready for use. Dip the brush and load it as heavily as possible, then brush it on thickly, as shown in the two photographs opposite, allowing the thick coating to lie over the entire surface. Test it occasionally to see how far penetration has occurred; when it has gone deeply, the finish can be removed. Loosened sludge can be washed or scraped off and if more paint remains to be removed, brush on another coat of remover and repeat the process. This type of powder remover works best on thick paints, not on clear finishes such as varnish.

BLEACHING OR BLANCHING WOOD

Sometimes bleaching or whitening wood is desirable or necessary, but not often. For real bleaching you must buy a prepared wood bleach that comes in a two-bottle package. Bottle #1 contains an alkaline water which could be drinking water with a small amount of lye added. Bottle #2 is strong commercial peroxide; make certain that you do not get any of it on your body. The photograph opposite shows how bottle #1 darkens wood. Immediately after a smooth darkening apply the peroxide and you will suddenly see that the action turns in the other direction, that is, toward white. Deep ink spots can be eradicated in this manner. See pages 81 and 82.

While oxalic acid is a bleach, it is really just a lightener. This is often useful in putting the appearance of "new life" into old wood. Of course, all bleaching is done with total disregard for patina.

When mixing oxalic crystals with water, prepare what is called a "saturate solution." You can get this by putting the crystals into the hottest water until no more of them will dissolve. Allow the mix to cool off before using. Remember that oxalic acid is poisonous internally, so after the desired lightening effect is achieved, wash off the wood thoroughly with water. See page 83.

REPAIRING VENEER

Veneering—thin sheets of fine woods—was often used to cover tops of tables, panels, and other parts of furniture; even drawers were sometimes lined with it in fine pieces of furniture. Occasionally it comes loose as water-soluble glues lose their pull because of humidity or dampness, as in the photograph opposite. Loose veneering must be carefully re-glued and put back in place before furniture can be properly refinished. If it is carefully done, no lines or seams will be noticeable when refinishing is completed.

METHOD. Loosen veneers and bend back carefully, loosening as far as necessary to reach gluing which holds. Carefully scrape off all particles of the old glue on the framework so that the rejoining will be as smooth and clean as possible. Put some white glue in the lid of a small tin can or other receptacle and use a small cheap paintbrush to apply glue to the area under the veneer, carefully bending veneer outward so that the brush can spread glue as far as possible behind it. Fit veneer exactly back into place and hold it tightly for a few minutes, to set the glue. Clean off any glue forced out of sides under the veneer and use a C-clamp with some strips of wood to protect veneer, or put a block of wood on veneer and weight it until glue has dried. *Make sure glue is well cleaned off before clamping or weighting,* or you will have glued the block to the veneer and be in even greater trouble. If the piece of loose veneer is small, it may be possible to hold it with the hands until it is sufficiently set and then clamp it for a moment or two within the next half hour, to keep it set.

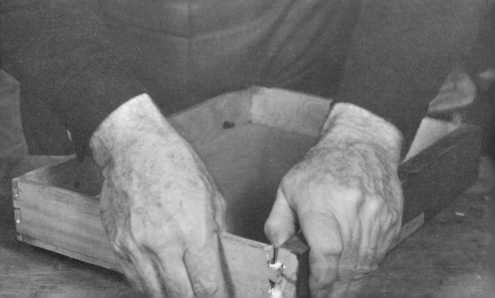

REPAIRS TO DOVETAILING

Because of the stress and strain of use, the dovetailing on the corners of drawers quite frequently loosens and finally parts company. The old glue becomes brittle and hard, no longer holding the two sides together; if allowed to go on for too long, the dovetailing becomes worn and may even split. Repair is necessary, and a good job will enable the drawer to be secure for a long, long time.

METHOD. Remove the side completely, as shown in the top photograph, working the dovetailing gently apart to avoid splitting the wood. Clean out all the old brittle pieces of glue from both parts of the dovetail joints, scraping it carefully away; clean out glue from the drawer bottom and the slot into which it fits, if the drawer is so constructed. Then, as shown in the bottom photograph, coat edges of dovetailing liberally with white glue and carefully put the two sides together again, fitting the dovetailing precisely. Make sure that the drawer is squared up and kept at a right angle while the glue is drying so that it will be foursquare and will pull in and out without binding. This is a good time, too, to check drawer runners, replacing them if they are worn, or coating them with a lubricant to keep them sliding easily. See pages 85 to 89.

DENTS IN FURNITURE

Quite frequently dents in wood can be raised enough so that they are hardly noticeable. Small ones may be repaired completely. If the wood fibers along the edges of the dent are not broken or badly damaged, it is often possible to put enough life back into the cells by the use of heat and moisture.

METHOD. First, remove all finish from the wood and clean the area around the dent, then moisten the wood and let it soak in well. Moisten a piece of heavy cloth or Turkish towel, place it over the dent, and then put a hot iron on the spot. Lift it and then press down again for a few minutes. Inspect the wood to see if the steam has "exploded" the cells that were crushed down and forced them to spring up again. If not, repeat the process. Unless the dent is quite deep, this will probably raise the wood to the surface or near it. Sanding paper rubbed over the area will remove any roughness which might have been induced and also help to bring the surface to a level. See page 87 for further details on repair of dents.

REBUILDING REPAIRS

Table top with a part of the raised lip broken away has been repaired by building up as directed in the text. The closeup shows repair before being toned and stained to blend into color of the wood and refinishing. The broken spot is just above the right side of the pedestal. After being stained, refinished, and waxed, the broken spot and its repair will be barely noticed, or, if cleverly done, indistinguishable from surrounding wood.

METHOD. Mix a small quantity of epoxy glue and then mix the glue with fine sawdust or wood powder, until you have a stiff mastic. Fill patch, in fact overfill slightly, molding with fingers. Allow about three days for curing, then sand back to proper shape and touch with stains for matching. Epoxy makes a very strong bond and the patch should last for the lifetime of the article.

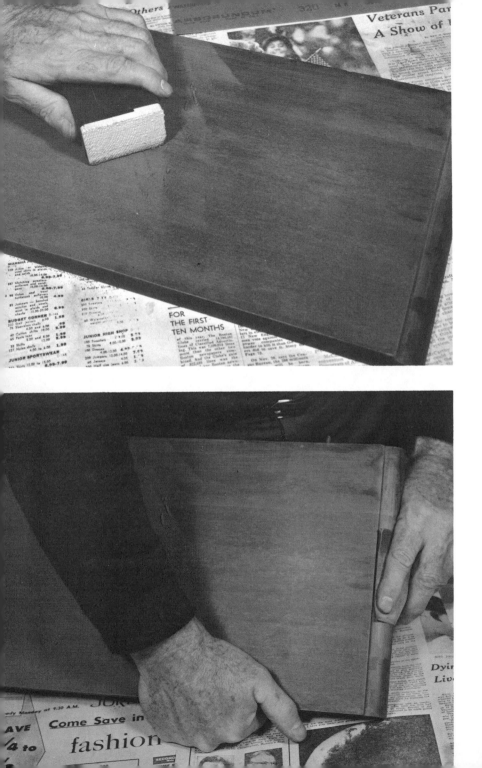

SURFACE SMOOTHING

After the finish has been removed and there is nothing but bare wood—or as close to bare wood as you can achieve with finish removers—all surfaces must be made smooth and ready to accept final finish coats. Much of the success of the refinishing depends upon this vital step.

METHOD. Use sanding papers for smoothing flat surfaces, starting with a medium grade if there is any roughness to tone down, a fine grade if it is relatively smooth when the hand is passed over the surface. Fold the paper around a block of wood (see top photograph, opposite) so that it can be held and used easily. Rub *with the grain* of the wood on flat surfaces, not across it or you may scratch and break the fibers and leave marks that will show under final finish. Keep large flat surfaces as horizontal as possible when sanding so that proper pressure control can be maintained. Boxlike large pieces—chests of drawers, desks, chests, dressers, and the like—may be turned as each successive side is smoothed. Maintain a fairly even pressure over all, and watch out for edges so that they are not sanded down and made rounded or some character may be lost. After sanding, wipe away dust and examine all surfaces to make sure that all parts have been covered; if any have been missed, or have resisted sanding, re-sand. Sometimes a piece of sandpaper furled around the index finger will clean a small resistant area quickly and more easily than by using a block and sanding paper. Again, work *with the grain of the wood*. Give a final polishing with very fine sanding paper and check again for smoothness and full coverage of all surfaces. Curved surfaces, such as table edges (see bottom photograph), are best smoothed by a piece of fine emery paper held firmly against the curve with the hand and rubbed back and forth gently. Use only *fine grades* of abrasive and exert only *gentle* pressure so as not to destroy the form of the curve and to prevent putting deep scratches, since this is often sanding *across* the grain.

SMOOTHING RUNGS AND ROUNDS

Always be sure that all parts of pieces are smoothed before they are refinished—even rungs, spindles, and legs need smoothing after the finish has been removed, so that they can accept the new finish. Sometimes it is difficult to get into cracks and crevices in turnings and these may need special attention; but for ordinary round pieces—rungs, legs, and smooth spindles—there is an easy method to remove the remains of any finish and smooth the pieces down to raw wood.

METHOD. Cut a piece of emery cloth about an inch wide—less than an inch if you must get into tiny crevices in turnings—and as long as the sheet of emery cloth. Furl this around the spindle, grasp one end in each hand, and work back and forth gently, keeping the pressure even by holding the cloth fairly taut. A moderate pressure will quickly and effectively make the rounded piece beautifully smooth. For larger rounds, such as legs that are not turned or ornamented, a piece of sanding paper of medium grade, followed by a fine grade for final smoothing, can be held in the hand and worked up and down on the leg until the desired smoothness is reached. For difficult corners and crevices, such as areas around joints where rungs are inserted into legs or spindles enter seats of chairs, emery boards used for filing fingernails may be employed effectively, for they can be inserted easily and their abrasives brought into contact with the surfaces to be smoothed far more effectively than with sanding papers or emery cloth on a finger, for instance.

NOTE. This is one of a pair of antique bow-back Windsor armchairs. They were badly weathered, but I picked them up for nothing and then reminded myself that extra work would be worthwhile. They were worth a complete hand-sanding job. Notice the wood splits, too, which were well taken care of with epoxy glue and clamps. Both chairs are now in good solid condition and in full use. I am glad to have saved two more orphans from the storm!

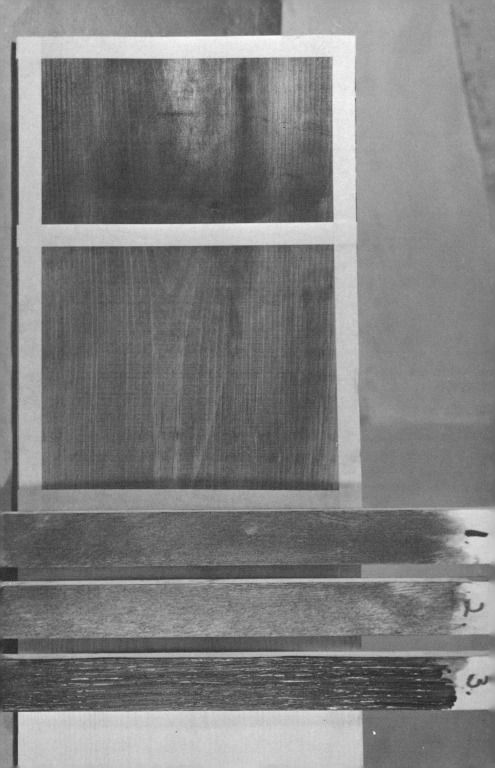

STAINING WOOD

Before stains are applied to any new woods of a porous nature, such as pine, whitewoods, fir, and mahogany, a coat of shellac diluted with alcohol (see page 106) should be brushed on to give a partial seal to the pores. Otherwise too much stain may be absorbed, or certain parts may accept the stain more readily than others, and the natural beauty of the wood graining may be obscured by the blotched results.

OPPOSITE. The photograph shows a pine board, the upper portion of which was stained without a shellac coat while the lower portion of it was stained after the diluted shellac had been applied. The horizontal pieces also demonstrate the results of staining. The top one was stained without the sealing coat of shellac, while #2 was given a diluted shellac coat before it was stained. Note how even and clear are the results of both examples which were stained after sealing, and how blotchy and uneven or cloudy are the results on the unsealed woods. The #3 board shows how a piece of stained wood can be given a change of graining by the use of two colors—first the regular stain, followed by a wiping on of color-in-oil. This gives the wood a bit more character than it would otherwise possess, a useful trick to know at times. See page 169 for further examples of staining.

WIPING ON WOOD STAINS

Wood can be toned to any shade you desire, from completely natural—a clear finish applied on unstained wood will darken it only slightly—to deep, rich, dark tones. Also, wood can be toned to red, brown, yellowish hues, or other colors may be applied to give a variety of coloration. See pages 100 to 103 for full details.

METHOD. Check the wood to be sure it is truly smooth and in condition to accept the stain. Wear rubber gloves and old clothes, even an apron if you wish, to keep the hands clean and to avoid getting spotted. Make up the stain solution (page 101) and put it in an old drinking glass or wide-mouthed jelly glass. Apply it with a folded cloth pad, using strokes *with the grain* of the wood, giving complete coverage and not leaving pools anywhere. If any blobs show up, blot them or rub them off with a clean dry cloth. If, after first stain coat is rubbed on and dry you feel it is too light (remember that it will darken only slightly if a clear finish is applied), give it a second coat after the first one is well dried. Use the stain thinned down and thin again for the second coat if only a light increase in color is indicated.

I use oil stains and believe it is part of the fun of refinishing to experiment and develop one's own stain colors, as I suggest in the text. Always be sure to make up enough to do the entire piece; even throw some away or bottle it for future use, rather than risk running out and not being able to match the color exactly for the second batch.

STAINING SPECIAL PARTS

Many parts of furniture do not lend themselves to easy application of stains and may need special attention to insure even coverage. Rather than take a chance on overcovering or underpigmentation of the wood in carvings, on deep crevices of turnings on rungs and spindles or legs, apply stain with a small paintbrush rather than depending on application with the wipe-on rag. Keep the brush moist with stain but do not overload it.

METHOD. Brush carefully in the deep parts of the crevices, making sure to cover all parts. Pick up any dribbles or drops with the brush so that not too much remains. Do only a small section at a time and then blot up any pools or drops with a soft, clean cloth. Rubber gloves, of course, should be worn for this operation. Place the chair or other piece of furniture so that it is in good light and, if possible, so that it can be turned easily to allow you to see what you are doing and the work can be done better.

Round legs or portions between turnings can usually be covered adequately with the wipe-on rag pad, holding it in the hand and bringing it into contact with the rounded parts as it is rubbed up and down. Always check around leg or seat holes where spindles, rungs, and other parts enter, making sure that they are covered. The small brush will be used there, too, to insure coverage.

SEALING WITH SHELLAC

Open-grained woods may need sealing. See text, pages 104 to 109, for details. Shellac is a good sealer, and is very easy to apply. Thin down as advised in the text before using it.

METHOD. Mix a solution of shellac and denatured alcohol in the proportions suggested on page 106 and place it in an old drinking glass or wide-mouthed jelly glass. Make sure the shellac is thoroughly dissolved, stirring it to mix, and make sure there are no lumps. Wear rubber gloves and old clothes for the job. Use a flat brush two to three inches wide to apply the shellac, brushing it on quickly and easily, covering the wood completely with the thin coat. Avoid overlapping strokes to prevent buildups. Shellac will dry quickly and be ready within a short time for further finishing work. A more uniform coverage of stains will result on certain woods if they also have this shellac sealing coat before being stained.

Examine the wood after the shellac is dry. If by any chance the fibers are roughed up and make slightly rough spots in the shellac finish, a piece of fine steel wool rubbed over them will cut down to the surface these prickly bits that stick up. Sometimes parts are missed in sanding to smooth and this is the best time to give the final smoothing before finish coats.

FINISHING COATS

After the wood stain sealer has thoroughly dried and met with your approval, it is time for the finishing coat. See pages 110 to 114 for guidance in selecting the finish you wish. Be sure that the piece is well wiped and free from dust or any foreign matter that would affect the finish. Since this is the final part of refinishing, this is the final coat, the one that you will see daily from now on. Be sure to do the refinishing in a dust-free atmosphere and that no dust is raised for several hours or until the finish is really dry.

METHOD. Place the piece in good light so that you can see what you are doing, to be certain of achieving complete and even coverage. Place flat surfaces as nearly horizontal as possible. With large boxlike pieces, do a side at a time, turning after each side is dry. Small pieces should be held conveniently so that they can be worked on and turned at will to achieve complete, even coverage, as shown with the chair, opposite. Use the varnish right out of the can; avoid shaking the can or stirring too vigorously lest bubbles be raised in the varnish which would be difficult to brush out in the finish. Keep the brush well covered but do not load it. Apply varnish with strokes *along the grain* of the wood. On edges, where you must work across the grain, avoid buildup of varnish. Watch for pools or overcoverage and pick up excesses quickly with the brush. (See page 117.) Allow finish to dry very hard before putting on succeeding coats. Several coats of thinned-down varnish are preferable to one coat of thick varnish, for the buildup means added strength and resiliency.

CLEANING AND WAXING: THE FINAL FINISH

After the last coat of varnish or paint has been thoroughly dried and smoothed, it is well to protect the surface with a good coating of hard paste wax. See page 124 for full details. This can be renewed as often as needed, but a properly applied paste-wax finish put on immediately after refinishing will not need renewal for a long, long time.

METHOD. Wax comes in colorless and also in brown-toned types. Apply it with a pad of soft cloth folded into a convenient size for the hand. Rub the wax on thinly, but uniformly, being sure it covers every part of the surface. Allow it to dry for ten or fifteen minutes and then give it a good sheen by rubbing it with a pad of #000 fine steel wool, as shown in the photograph opposite; the friction created by the lightly held pad will help to melt the wax and make a hard surface. Two or three waxings within the first few weeks after refinishing will build up a good hard-wax finish that will last wonderfully well. Possibly once a year you may go over it again. However, such a finish needs little care and gives excellent protection.

Old furniture in regular use, but smudged from various applications of cheap, quick, oil or silicone shines, may be washed down with paint thinner and then hard paste-waxed, as shown in these photographs. Preserve your furniture better and have less work to do in the polishing arena for all time to come.

SPATTERING TO DECORATE

Spatterwork in a single color or in several colors is an interesting means of decorating. It is an old craft, having been much used on painted, wide-boarded floors in bedrooms and other rooms of old farmhouses. It has also been adapted to use for table tops, and as a means of decorating dressers, chests of drawers, blanket chests, and so on. It simulates marble or stone, if more than one color is used, and is often used as a groundwork for hand-veining with a brush in true marbleizing.

METHOD. See pages 132 and 133 where spattering is covered at length. Basically the method is to load a paintbrush, a whisk broom, a toothbrush, or any other stiff-bristled brush with a fair amount of color. By tapping the ferrule of the brush against a stick of wood, hitting the whisk brush or other stiff-bristled brush sharply against a piece of wood, or by springing the stiff bristles of a toothbrush so that they cast their load of paint in droplets, blobs and drops will fall and spatter on the object to be decorated. Try out the process before attempting the final work so as to get the hang of the craft and to see what effects you can get. Use a piece of pasteboard carton, a piece of old board, or plain wrapping paper held flat. Any odds and ends of paint may be used, whether oil or water emulsible, and you may want to see what tools get the best effect for you. A toothbrush naturally will cast small droplets, while the coarser the bristles the larger will be the drops when using other kinds of brushes. A whisk broom is coarsest of all. Several colors may be used, one spattering on top of another. I have used only one color to demonstrate spatterwork on the photographed board opposite. Spatter dark colors on light backgrounds, light ones on dark backgrounds, bright spatters on dull-colored backgrounds, and dull colors or black on bright painted pieces. Allow spattering to dry well for two or three days before giving a thin coat or two of varnish to protect it from wear.

PICKLED OR LIMED WOOD

An interesting way to bring out the natural graining in open-pored woods such as oak, pine, walnut, and certain of the mahoganies is a method known as "pickling." Basically all this means is that a color (usually white or a color lighter than the woods) is brushed on, then wiped across the grain and wiped off, leaving the wood pores filled with the color and often a light silvery effect in the smaller pores which gives a different and unusual appeal to the finish. When bleached wood is treated similarly, the finish is called "limed." Pickled pine, pickled mahogany, and pickled walnut have been popular of late years, and limed-oak finishes are often used on modern pieces as well as for refinishing old ones.

METHOD. If you wish a dark tone on the wood, wipe on the stain before pickling and let it dry well. Paint may also be used as the base coat if it is well thinned before application, so that it does not fill the pores. After the base coat is thoroughly dry, brush on the color you have chosen for the pickling, covering the piece roughly and well. Wipe the pigment across the grain to force it well into the grain, then continue to wipe with clean cloths until all of the color except that remaining in the pores is removed. Brushing *with the grain* will scoop out the paint and none will be left, so wipe *across the grain* always. Allow to dry well, then protect with a coat of varnish, or several coats of wax if this effect is used only on the frame of an upholstered piece. The photograph opposite demonstrates an unpickled painted board above, with a painted board after pickling below. Note how the grain is brought out and emphasized.

OTHER EFFECTS. Limed oak can be first bleached as light as possible, then white paint wiped into the pores, as above, and wiped off. Bleached mahogany can be wiped with white filler, a red-toned filler, or a natural beige-toned filler, each giving a different effect. Walnut can be lightly stained with a thinned-down brown stain, then a light color is wiped across the grain.

GRAINING AND MARBLEIZING

Both of these techniques, illustrated opposite, are valuable at times for various uses. Graining can give considerable interest to a flat piece of wood with no grain or an uninteresting grain. In both cases shown the effects have been exaggerated in order to demonstrate how the strokes should be applied. A more subtle final effect is to be desired in both cases.

METHOD. Left, marbleizing of a very rudimentary sort suitable for country-style furniture and other unsophisticated uses. It is not to be confused with the kind of marbleizing that reproduces real marble veining with a paintbrush. Such skillful marbleizing is used for sophisticated French and other furniture, where true marble would be too heavy or too expensive. The sort shown here merely gives interest to an otherwise dull, painted surface. First apply the base coats of paint and allow them to dry thoroughly. I used a dark green base with a light green-gold paint applied and allowed it to set for a few minutes until it flattened out and began to set but was still rather liquid. The surface was then wiped with a piece of crumpled newspaper. Any stroke you use to get the desired effect is up to you—straight, circular, curving strokes, or combinations. Allow the scoring of the paper to show in the paint —do not wipe it all off or mostly off, though in some places the coat may be thinned by the stroke. Try practicing a bit before you start on a big piece of work; use scrap pieces of wood painted the base color and get the technique in your wrist and arm so that you will approach the final job confidently.

The photograph on the right shows the effect of straight strokes which resemble wood graining. Paper may be crumpled loosely or closely; a piece of rough Turkish towel, a dry synthetic sponge, or other materials may also be used. All are useful, and you may develop other techniques with practice. There are no limitations except imagination and experience in this technique. On oak and other heavily grained woods, gold or silver is sometimes wiped into the grain pores; it is particularly handsome on black or other dark-colored, painted backgrounds. For tables and other wearing surfaces, it is wise to protect the pickling or liming with a coat or two of varnish, clear and strong.

RESCUE WORK

Once the original scarred finish was removed, an old chest of drawers (photograph opposite) was found to be constructed of inferior woods with bad grains. It might have been painted a solid color and used that way, but in this case it was decided that graining would add to the interest and give it more character.

The drawer pulls were removed to be finished separately and the drawers were taken out and placed upright so that the front could be worked on horizontally, making the finishing easier. After smoothing and preparing all surfaces, the base coat of paint was applied and allowed to dry thoroughly. The contrasting color chosen for the graining coat was then brushed on roughly and, after being allowed to set for a short time, while it was still wet enough to work the graining was done.

Graining here was done with a roughly wadded newspaper, but it can also be done with rough cloths, dry synthetic sponges, or brushes. See page 130. Keep removing paint with the paper, cloth, sponge, or brush until you have achieved the desired effect. You can make "worn" corners by wiping a little more heavily on them. Brush or wipe off drawer pulls, too. Allow to dry, then apply a protective coat or two of varnish which will tone down and pull the graining effect together. Attach the drawer pulls when everything is dry and the chest is ready for use.

In the photograph only part of the chest of drawers is finished, to demonstrate the direction of the graining, and to show what can be done. The grain, however, has been emphasized, so that it would show in the photograph. A more subtle effect should be striven for.

EMPHASIZING DETAILS

In order to bring out a bit of carving, a well-defined molding, or some other detail of the furniture, antiquing can be used. Even if the furniture is not painted but finished with a clear finish to show the wood grain, such antiquing can be effective. On painted furniture, of course, this is much used to give a mellowness. A darker tone is applied over a well-dried finish coat of paint, allowed to set for a short time, then wiped off, leaving the high spots of the carving wiped dry of the antiquing color, but the low spots shaded down to the deeper crevices which may have almost full strength of the darker antiquing tone, such shadings simulating the darkening and use that comes with age.

OPPOSITE. In the photograph I have used a very light color to make my point clear—probably much lighter than you would want to have it in your antiquing—and this kind of "reverse antiquing," or filling of depressions and crevices with a lighter color may also be used to enhance and bring out carvings on dark-toned pieces. If the base color was dark brown, a lighter brown can be brushed on, then wiped off, leaving the high spots with little or no added color, the low spots shaded with the wiping. For instance, if a different color scheme was employed, a greenish-gold can be applied over a darker green; bone white can be applied on grays or other colors; blue can be placed over darker, duller blues; and pink tones can be put over browns of umber or sienna shades. Gold picture frames with carved or ornamented moldings can be particularly effective when antiqued with dull, dark colors—Burnt Umber, Raw Umber, and shades of green are used most effectively. Some refinishers use subdued tones of pink, blue, or green to bring out carvings on natural wood finishes, but this is certainly not authentic, however pleasant the results may be.

STENCIL WORK

The pair of chairs in the photograph opposite show how much a simple little stencil adds to the looks of furniture. For inspiration consult books showing antiques with such designs and copy or adapt them, or, if you are so inclined, make your own designs. Follow the method outlined in this book under Stencils, pages 134 to 135, making the stencil of architects' tracing linen cloth, working on the shiny side, with dull side down. You may want to use the same stencil on a number of pieces—note the drawer front in the lower photograph, as well as the chairs.

METHOD. You will need bronzing powder in whatever shade or shades of gold you wish, or perhaps silver will please you for this purpose. Stencils may also be painted or done in color.

Once the stencil is ready you can begin. Apply a coat of varnish to the area to be decorated and allow it to dry until it is tacky. Lay the piece of furniture down so that the part to be stenciled is horizontal. Press the stencil on the varnish (with dull side down) in the exact position you wish to have it appear. Press down firmly, especially around the cut edges, to make it adhere and not allow any gold powder to get under it. Wrap a scrap of velvet around your forefinger, dip the velvet lightly into gold bronzing powder, and then gently tap and pat on the gold in the area of the stencil you want to cover. With care, you can get shading from dark to light, to give a three-dimensional look to the design. I have also used ordinary cloth, and even my bare fingertip, to apply the gold, smearing as well as tapping it into the varnish.

When the cutout areas have been covered to your satisfaction, carefully lift off the stencil after brushing and gather up any excess powder. Clean the stencil with paint thinner so that it can be used again when it dries. After the stenciled decoration is thoroughly dry, protect it with a coat of varnish.

FREEHAND DECORATION

Often a piece that is not otherwise distinguished can be made interesting and useful by being decorated with designs, either hand-painted or stenciled. (See page 134 for Stenciling.) In the photograph opposite we show some freehand innovations. Many amateurs can sketch a pansy, a cloverleaf, a daisy, or can improvise an arabesque or other pleasing pattern on articles that might otherwise be headed for the junk heap. Such old-fashioned things as coal hods can be decorated and used as wood baskets for fireplaces or for magazines and other paraphernalia. Sometimes a not-too-good carving can be enhanced with clever brushwork, minimizing the bad points, bringing up the good ones, and adding design around the edges or extending and beautifying the pattern present.

Bright or subtle colors, gold, and silver are all good to use, keying the colors to the job and the design to be used.

METHOD. Work out the design idea first, then paint it freehand or trace the design on with chalk or grease pencil first. The base coat of paint, of course, must be applied first and allowed to dry before you decorate the surfaces. Allow the decorations to dry for at least a day before protecting with one or two coats of thinned varnish.

REMODEL FOR NEW USES

Victorian marble-topped tables are coming into favor again and new uses are being found for them in today's homes. As chairside tables they are refinished and used as they are but for other uses they may be remodeled and cut down, as shown in the photograph.

ABOVE. When refinished, the tall table is ready to give flavor to the living-room scene. But it is twenty-eight inches high. For the lowslung furniture of today—sofas and other upholstered pieces—this height is inconvenient. When cut down to coffee-table height it is in better proportion for the use it should serve, and this can be done without altering the proportions unpleasantly. The marble top and fine wood apron that supports it will remain the same—only the legs and pedestal are cut. This is relatively easy to do.

BELOW. Most pedestals and leg sections are attached to the top by screws. Lift off the marble top and put it in a safe place. Upend the table and remove the screws from the wooden apron section. Place leg section upright on a level floor and determine the height you desire table top when cut down. Subtract thickness of marble and of the supporting member under it (center board of apron section) and using a yardstick firmly based on the floor and held tightly to each leg and to the pedestal, mark the height. Saw off legs and pedestal carefully; all must be of same height or the top will not be level. Sink long screws through center support into each leg and pedestal. Refinish all wood parts, replace marble top, and table is ready for use.

MAKING AND REMAKING ANTIQUES

Repairing antiques or making up your own antiques from odd bits and pieces is part of the fun for the amateur craftsman. A little ingenuity plus an eye that sees possibilities in broken or thrown-away objects is all that is required. At left in the photograph opposite is a useful little chairside piece to hold knitting or any other oddments. The top was a discarded wooden bowl and the base was a broken pedestal from an old tabouret. Cut down to proper height it makes a sturdy base for the bowl. The inside of the bowl was finished to show the natural wood grain, the outside and base were painted black, decorated with gold. The other little table was a wobbly old flower stand. Re-glued and refinished, fitted with an antique box and cup plate to serve as an ashtray, and painted black with hand decorations in gold, it has a new use.

Often pieces are discarded when some part is broken. An antique rocker for a child might need a spindle, a rung, or a rocker replaced. Most home craftsmen could copy a spindle on a lathe (or a local professional could do it) and when it is refitted, the piece can be stained to match the rest of the wood or the whole piece painted to bring it into harmony. It can then be put to good use and preserved for future generations to enjoy.

PART IV

Further Notes

THE HOME WORKSHOP

Although it is not necessary to have a workshop in which to refinish furniture, as proved by many an antiquer who has redone even sizable pieces in a small apartment, it is certainly an asset if one is going to do a number of pieces and if the room is available. As small a spot in the basement or garage as five feet by eight feet can be functional and quite adequate. The main requirements are that there should be good heat, good ventilation, cleanliness, and a good drying atmosphere that is free from dust. Dust is the enemy of newly applied finishes as they dry. Warmth is most essential for the proper application and drying of the various finish coats. A workshop should be kept at 65 degrees to 75 degrees F. as the minimum. Dampness is a hazard and the atmosphere should be dry, to overcome attendant handicaps associated with humidity. Never use any commercial liquid paint remover (and some of the synthetic sealers) unless really good ventilation is available.

The refinisher's workshop should be kept clean at all times, so that it will be eternally dust free. Probably at some auction you can bid on and buy a secondhand vacuum cleaner cheaply. It is not necessary to have an elaborate setup with all the gadgets going—you can assemble them one by one as they are needed and as they are useful for the job in hand. If the object is to set up a small shop and begin to refinish furniture as a retirement business, then of course you will want to have more tools and gadgets than you might otherwise buy. That is, by the way, a very pleasant occupation for one's older years, either as a pin-money business conducted at one's own pace and in one's own time, or as a hobby to occupy one's time and delight one's ego. Some retired people begin by refinishing furniture for themselves, and soon graduate to doing it for their friends, or they find an antiques dealer who will use their services or recommend them to his customers. Doing the work as one finds the time or as the work comes in is a pleasant way to spend the retirement years. Buying antiques at auctions or from combing the shops, junk yards, dumps, or the other places recommended may also be useful in setting up a small "business" of trading in antiques. Finding them and restoring them, then charging a reasonable markup and selling them can be a most absorbing and pleasing hobby-business.

For the small home workshop you will need fixing tools—hammers and screwdrivers of various sizes and kinds, pliers, knives, several saws, files, planes, drills, and many other small, useful hand tools. The kind and the number depend upon how deeply you want to get involved in repairs—and, of course, your skill in repairing. You will need glues, too, of course.

For refinishing only, you need basically only the following:

FOR FINISH REMOVAL
    Paint removers
    Old paintbrush or brushes
    Coffee can
    Rubber gloves (heavy, lined)
    Rubber apron (useful but not mandatory)
    Rags, coarse and rough, fine and soft
    Mineral spirits
    Denatured alcohol
    Small fiber brush, stiff bristled

Small, soft, metal-bristled brush (wire brush)
Steel wool, coarse (#3 grade)
Trisodium phosphate (TSP)
Heavy-duty laundry detergent
Putty knife or scraper

FOR SMOOTHING WOOD

Silicone carbide papers (wet or dry type) in medium, fine, very fine grades
Steel wool (#000 and #00 grades)
Prepared natural-color wood filler
Emery cloth, fine and very fine grades
Old paintbrush

FOR STAINING WOOD

Stain in various colors as needed
Rubber gloves
Work apron, rubber or other type
Mineral spirits
Lint-free cloths

FOR FINISHING WOOD

Furniture varnishes, good quality only
Mineral spirits and/or
Turpentine
Boiled linseed oil
New (or *clean*) varnish brushes, 2 inches or 3 inches wide
Small, round-ferrule paintbrushes for small spots
Steel wool (#000 and #00 grades)
Silicone carbide paper (wet or dry type) fine, very fine grades
Shellac
Denatured alcohol
Tinting colors

FOR POLISHING

Paste wax, hard carnauba type, colorless and/or dark brown
Soft cloths for application
Steel wool (#000 grade)

Once you have as many of these things as you need to get started, you are on your way. It is helpful to have a heavy, solid workbench on which to support your work as you do the various tasks, from repairing to the final refinishing. A bench that is six to seven feet in length and two to three feet wide, according to the space available and the needs you have, is adequate. In height, a good bench might be thirty to thirty-two inches for shorter people, thirty-six to thirty-eight inches for taller workers. A wood vise is also a good tool to possess, and often is better than a hired hand to hold things as you work on them. You may not need to build a workbench—you may find one at a country auction, or on that town dump, that you can have for the taking. You can often pick up excellent used tools at auctions, too, and for very little money.

Now that the workshop is outlined, you can choose what course you want to follow, how deeply you want to enter into the pursuit of the hobby of refinishing antiques in the common-sense way.

SHOPPING FOR SUPPLIES?
LET'S GO TOGETHER!

Inasmuch as I have kept this book as free as possible from commercials, I believe that my service to you would not be complete until I offered some suggestions for saving you time and money as you search for and select the proper products that are needed in common-sense furniture refinishing. Under no circumstances do I have any desire or reason to favor any supplier or manufacturer, but I will use certain manufacturing or brand names when I know that their use will be worthwhile to you. What I offer here comes from personal experience only, and is in no way any reflection on any names that are not included.

The following products can be readily purchased from any reliable hardware or paint store. Depend on whatever your favorite dealer stocks in these items:

BASICS

Bronzing powders	Paints and enamels
Contact papers	Peroxide wood bleach
Denatured alcohol	Two-tube epoxy gluing system
Lacquer thinner	Varnish and paintbrushes
Oxalic crystals	White glue in plastic bottles
Paint thinner	Wood filler (plain or colored)
Turpentine	

STEEL WOOL.   #3 is very coarse and may be best for the stripping job. #2 is a little finer. Stock both. For all smoothing jobs, stock #00 and #000, #000 being the preferred and the finest. Buy in pads that come in boxed units.

RUBBER GLOVES. They should be heavy and cloth backed. The best for wear is made of neoprene or vinyl. Get extra large sizes so they go on and off easily.

ARCHITECT'S LINEN. For stenciling. Found in better artist's supply shops.

TRISODIUM PHOSPHATE (TSP). Every store stocked it at one time, as the favored professional heavy-duty cleaner. Some stores may not have it now. I know that Sears, Roebuck sells it as a packaged item, under the name TSP.

SANDING PAPERS. I hope that your dealer is up-to-date, so that he stocks the "wet-or-dry" silicone carbide papers. Also, that he stocks emery cloth and the very fine crocus cloth.

OIL COLORS IN TUBES. You can make your own stains with paint thinner, if you wish. I refer to the earth colors, such as the umbers and siennas, plus the black, red, and blue, and just be sure that there is no confusion with the ordinary "paint-tinting colors" which also come in tubes. You want artist's colors-in-oil and not paint-tinting colors. In this case, to be certain, I suggest the name *Grumbacher*. Good art supply stores have it.

WOOD STAINS. The ready-mixed type. Get the least pigmented brand. Rely upon an experienced clerk's advice. Purchase the basic shades and intermix them in your workshop for your own particular shades. There are thousands of stain names and hundreds of stain brands. Do not buy or use stains already mixed into penetrating sealers or finishes.

LIQUID PAINT REMOVERS. Purchase quality at a quality store. Rely upon the dealer to supply the best *nonflammable* and *heavy-bodied* type. There are scores of brand names and many manufacturers.

SHELLAC. Purchase small quantities. Shellac will deteriorate; if it is as much as a year old, it may never dry. Use only white or colorless liquid shellac.

CARNAUBA PASTE WAX. Make sure it contains *carnauba* wax and that the dealer signifies it is quality. If it contains carnauba wax, the manufacturer will be proud to say so on the label. One of the best, and perhaps the oldest brand, it can be purchased for less than a dollar in a one-pound can. A newer, competing brand that is widely advertised sells for about twice as much. Look twice and inquire. High cost does not necessarily signify the best purchase in this item.

VARNISHES. For fine furniture finishing. There are many good brands. However, there are two brand names that are generally well known and accepted and I hereby mention them as *Valspar* and as *McClosky*. These two manufacturers are specialists in finishes and they employ the favored tung oil, alkyd, or soya resins. They make high-gloss, semi-gloss, sheens, and flats. Whatever you purchase, read the labels first, as to what resins they do contain and whether or not the varnish can be thinned with paint thinner.

FOR ADDITIONAL KNOWLEDGE. If you wish to go further into the business of stripping and refinishing furniture, it is true that the professional has access to much more efficient and easier ways to strip on a larger scale. For instance, most professionals make use of a much "wetter" and completely water emulsifiable liquid paint remover and of simple mechanical means that help to produce a profit. There is a specific sludge remover available to the professional, although the ideas in this book are the best that can be made at home. There is also the powder paint-stripper. If you want more information, write to Pilot-House, P. O. Box 322, Marblehead, Massachusetts. For all kinds of refinisher's supplies, including veneering, send 25¢ for a most wonderful catalog that is produced by Albert Constantine & Son, Inc., 2050 Eastchester Road, Bronx, New York.

Thus, our shopping trip has come to an end.

SOME TIPS FOR ANTIQUERS

CLEANING BRASS OR PEWTER. Let the metal soak for a while in a mild solution of lye and water. Wear rubber gloves.

CLEANING COPPER. Make a paste of vinegar and salt. Rub the surface with a cloth that is loaded with this chemical mix.

CLEANING DIRTY CRACKS IN CHINAWARE. Soak overnight in bleach water.

CLEANING GLASSWARE. The best cleaner for glassware is water and ammonia. Glass will sparkle like new again. If you have a piece of glass that is dirty on the inside and the neck is too small for fingers or instruments, drop in some hard rice or pea beans. Add the ammonia water and shake vigorously.

CLEANING GOLD LEAF. Use only ammonia and water. Never use abrasives.

CLEAR WOOD FINISH SCRATCHES. Clean the scratch with a rubbing of paint thinner, or maybe a very light rub of fine sanding paper, such as emery or crocus cloth. Apply a touch of matching wood stain and let it dry. Lightly fill the crack with varnish, using a tiny pointed artist's brush, and let it dry. Rub the new varnish very lightly with a mixture of fine pumice and oil (most any oil). Then polish with hard paste carnauba wax polish. Some have used iodine, mercurochrome, or colored ink pencils for coloring the scratch. The quickest way, and it is often successful, is just to use similar colored shoe polish.

ELIMINATING WHITE RINGS ON CLEAR FINISHES. First, try wiping with full-strength ammonia. The fumes may remove the ring, which is on the surface. If not, try swiping with a cloth that is saturated with lacquer thinner. If the finish is lacquer, you should have success. Be nimble and do not swipe too much, as lacquer thinner will dissolve lacquer. If the finish is shellac, then swipe with a cloth saturated with alcohol. The alcohol will quickly remove the surface of the alcohol coating. Varnish rings are the most difficult to get rid of and that is because someone did not use the proper varnish. Good quality, modern furniture varnishes are not subject to white rings, as they can stand up under heat and water. Make up a paste of cigar ash and oil. Then, rub, rub, rub. If this fails, try a fine pumice-and-oil rub. Some claim a rub with turpentine will do it. If all these ideas fail, then the varnish should be completely removed with a paint and varnish remover, and the entire surface refinished.

FURNITURE, CARVED. Much of the carving is Oriental, but most of this kind of work was done in America.

FURNITURE, DECORATIVE. Old hand or stenciled decorations are valuable, whether perfect or not. They can be copied and duplicated. Do not destroy.

IDENTIFICATIONS ON FURNITURE. If there is a paper label glued on by an old clockmaker or cabinetmaker, do not remove it even though it may be partly destroyed.

MARBLE TOP IDENTIFICATIONS. The most valuable has fancy and scalloped edges. Second most valuable has slightly decorative corners. Least valuable has straight line edging. But all of it is valuable! As to color, values drop off as you go from reddish, rose, and brown, to blackish and then to white.

SIGNS OF ANTIQUITY IN FURNITURE. Round turnings, like bedposts, legs, and spindles, are apt to be quite irregular if they were turned out on real oldtime wood lathes. Machine turnings are regular and perfect, thus not so old. Early brasses and iron mounts were hand wrought irregularly, and not machine stamped perfectly. This is another sign of antiquity. Early American beds were never "single" or "twin" beds. In the olden days, only very large beds were used, for sleeping two or more. The only old individual small bed was a trundle bed (often on wheels), to sleep a small child. Thin, softwood pine backing on drawers and chests generally indicate that the article was American made. Perhaps there has been more "worm-hole" furniture made since 1920 than in all prior years. Worm holes do not indicate antiquity in manufacturing.

SOME ADDED FACTS
ABOUT FINISHES

Finishes vary greatly. There are thousands of mixes with just as many peculiarities. There are the so-called "clear" finishes, which consist largely of shellac, lacquer, and varnish. Then there are the colorful "pigmented" finishes, or paints. Paints consist mainly of the old milk paints, the casein paints, the oil or oil-and-lead paints, the paints with varnishes (enamels), and the water-emulsion paints which are mostly latex or synthetic rubber paints. There are also old, old furniture finishes that do not amount to much finish at all; here is a list of them with their approximate times in history.

DATING CLEAR-TYPE FINISHES

1600s	Hand grease and beeswax
1700s	Beeswax, oil, shellac
1800s	Oil and wax, shellac, varnish
1900s (early)	Shellac, varnish, oil lacquer and wax
1900s (late)	Same, plus vinyl, urethane, and other synthetics

DATING PIGMENTED PAINTS

1600s	Milk paints and hard whitewash
1700s	Milk and casein paint; water paint
1800s	Casein, lead and oil, enamels, tar (asphaltum)
1900s (early)	Oil and lead, enamel
1900s (late)	Alkyd resin, water emulsion latex, epoxy, and other synthetics

Note that I have indicated only the time of prime usage or popularity. Shellac is still used, for example, but in lesser and lesser quantities. Lead and oil paints are still in use, but the water-emulsion latex paints are fast cutting into this market. Since the introduction of lacquer in the 1920s, probably 90 per cent of our factory furniture has been lacquer coated. To simplify the chart for the new refinisher, the better type of commercial liquid-solvent paint removers are the best weapons to remove *all* of the finishes listed under "Clear-Type" and the twentieth-century concoctions listed under "Pigmented." The commercial liquid-solvent paint removers will not be found effective on old milk paints, nor very efficient on thick coatings of regular paints.

In the Old World, fine furniture was made only for royalty until about 1700. It was not coated with any of the finishes we use, not even shellac. The finish or patina came solely from hand sweat and nothing else but hand rubbing was permitted. It was not until the latter part of the 1600s that someone had the nerve to introduce a small quantity of oil and beeswax. Shellac was accepted toward the end of the seventeenth century, but it was invariably called "varnish." The word "varnish" goes back to King Tut's time, but such "varnishes" were in no way related to the present-day varnish. Modern varnish came along in the nineteenth century. Modern lacquer is less than fifty years old, strictly a twentieth-century invention. If you plan to collect good furniture that was made in the late 1600s to the middle 1700s in the New World, expect to find that the original finish was linseed oil, beeswax, or possibly shellac. Around the time of the Civil War varnished furniture was produced, but practically all of the mass-produced furniture since 1925 is lacquered.

Historically, we learn that "lacquer" is varnish or shellac, that "shellac" is *lakker* or lacquer, and that "varnish" is shellac or lacquer. Will the real shellac, lacquer, or varnish please stand up? *Lakker*, made from the sap of the Japanese varnish tree, was used in Oriental craftwork many centuries ago. It was not in any way like the lacquer of today. Our lacquers stem from synthetic chemical compounds, beginning with a highly toxic and explosively flammable nitrocellulose invented by a Mr. Flaherty in 1921. Shellac is a resinous excretion from an insect that is native to the Far East. The dried excretion is dissolved in alcohol, a method for making shellac since the 1700s. Varnish, as we know it today, is another product of the chemical laboratory, being basically a compounding of china wood oil, phenolics, gums, resins, and driers.

Paints go back so far in time that no one could give a date for their birth. It is anyone's guess, five thousand to one hundred and five thousand years ago. We are concerned with something new like antiques, however, so we need not care about paints put on before the time of our American ancestors about three hundred years ago. Even in this comparatively short period of time there are thousands of different paint mixes, plus thousands of fetching brand names that have been unfurled on metal paint cans in the past century. It might be easier to start with today and go backward. First, let's put modern paints into two classifications: the water-emulsion paints which are not airtight coatings and the oil paints which are mostly airtight and not water emulsible. When you hear about acrylic, butyl, latex, polyvinyl acetate, you are hearing about water-emulsion paints. When you hear about enamel, oil and lead, alkyd resin, oil, aluminum, chlorinated rubber, you are being told about paints that are airtight and do not "breathe."

I definitely prefer water-emulsion paints, except when a hard gloss is desired. The nonwater paints are slow drying and especially on exterior work I do not appreciate a generous sprinkling of dead bugs. These oil paints are often smelly and sticky and they always cause a lot of cleanup trouble. They cannot be properly applied unless the weather has been perfectly dry for days and unless the article to be painted is bone dry, too. Without this dryness, oil paints will pop out in large blisters before a year's end. Colors in oil paints fade more quickly and matching is more difficult. Oil paints do not last long—a quality mix might survive five or six years under the best conditions. Oil paints form a positive moisture barrier, and right there you have the makings of those blisters. Should someone ask me if I believe that one hundred years of oil-and-lead painting outdoors has led us down a path of needless ills, I would have to reply, "Ayah, I shorely think so." And that is why I am glad that the paint manufacturing industry has come back to water-emulsion paints.

The modern water-emulsion paints breathe, just like fine paints of years and years ago. The old boys were not so stupid after all! If the base that you are painting on is firm, then the water-base paint will not pop up in blisters. It will not fade out so quickly. It dries much quicker and does not snare the bugs. A little moisture one side or the other does not ruin your paint job later. Cleanup is much easier and much safer, and you eliminate all those expensive brush-cleaning solvents. Water is enough, if you do not allow the brush to dry out.

Working backward in our paint history we find that most of the old homemade paints were water emulsible like our modern paints, except they did not contain valuable synthetic resins and were not in the best of colors. They were often nothing more than skimmed milk, lime, whiting, and ground color, but they let air in and out and that was the secret of their durability. They lasted long; in fact, some have held to the weather on barns for a half century or more. Others have firmly held on furniture for over two hundred years. I recently refinished a 1748 blanket chest that was covered only with original homemade paint of a light brick-red coloration. The condition was good, but it got stripped for other reasons. What modern paint is going to survive two centuries or more? This oldtime mixture is given several names: in antique circles you will hear about "milk paint," "buttermilk paint," "refractory paint." That last name—refractory—simply means "obstinate" and obstinate it is. Where is the commercial liquid paint remover that will dissolve it? Professional paint-strippers do not use such a remover; they use a modern powder mix that is specifically made for the purpose. Others claim that ammonia or sal soda will remove refractory paints that are ordinarily found on pieces of good country style furniture. I will bet a large jug full of the best old refractory paint against a pint of the best modern commercial liquid paint remover that the paint remover manufacturer cannot back up the statements on his labels.

Refractory paints are good clues to antiquity. If a commercial paint remover won't budge it after several applications and a wait of several hours, then you have found refractory paint. (Make a spot test.) If the paint does not have a shine or gloss and is either an off-white, faded brick-red, faded olive-green, brownish, or black color, that will be another clue. It could mean that the furniture is one hundred to two hundred years old. If it is in good shape, keep it the way it is. Excellent identity.

Thousands of people have made furniture, particularly during our early settler days, but there are few famous American cabinetmakers. Possibly Duncan Phyfe could be so classified. Hepplewhite, Chippendale, Sheraton—all were foreigners, but everyone in America copied them for styling. Many country lads with an honest eye, a flawless piece of wood, and a handiness with simple tools made fine furniture. The country cabinetmaker also painted much of his furniture. Some say he did so to cover up the fact that he used pine for the seat and birch for the legs, but I am certain he did so because he was also proud of his paint. When you become a stripper you will be amazed to uncover some of the finest woods beautifully fitted together in country furniture. I know many pieces of country furniture that excel some of the Hepplewhite and Chippendale craftsmanship of London.

The old is good, if not the best. That goes for paint as well as for furniture.

A NEW FURNITURE FINISH

Although new water emulsion paints and finishes always seem to have to survive through a childhood of hardships, many have gradually won acceptance by producing a better veneer than oil finishes. Modern indoor water emulsion, or latex paints have survived thirty years of testing against oil paints, and they now account for about ninety percent of all indoor decorating needs. (Outdoor top quality acrylic-latex house paints are also showing great superiority over the old oil paints—especially against cracking, blistering, peeling and color fading—and have already captured about fifty percent of the market; they will do even better as old habits wear away.) And, since the oil scare, believe it or not, you can now readily purchase a brand new polymerized or modified acrylic water emulsion clear finish for furniture that should do away with the need of the sticky, smelly, and humanly toxic oil varnishes of the past. Surely, the future would be much brighter if other industries, like the large paint manufacturing industry, could find ways of eliminating human hazards and at the same time become independent of oil and its resulting petrochemicals.

During the past couple of years, I have been carefully testing and comparing the progressive results of new clear water-base finishes from various protective coatings laboratories. At the start, I worked with original batches or samples of water-based clear finishes, only to have disappointment in test after test. Some of the pilot formulations dried out too quickly. Others would not self-level, leaving all the brush lines, and several others dried with a surface that was too soft for practical uses. Now, however, these problems have been solved and the public may readily purchase a clear, smooth, easy-to-apply, acrylic-latex, water-based clear finish. This finish flows on as easily as water, sets up a tremendous adhesive power, dries hard and usable within one hour, and becomes almost scratch-proof. In all ways, it shows attributes of excellence and should please every furniture refinisher on every level. Its advantages can be quickly summed up, as follows:

1. Can be applied over moist wood.
2. Will not craze, crack, chip, or peel.
3. Impervious to steam, heat, and alcohol.
4. Does not scratch easily.
5. Nonflammable and nontoxic.
6. No odors or fumes.
7. No tackiness or dust problems.
8. Absolutely clear and no wood discoloration.
9. Each coating dries within the hour.
10. Tools and hands can be cleaned with soap and water.

Acrylic resins and water are the vehicles, replacing oils and petrochemicals. Be sure, when purchasing, to read the container label carefully, as there are other types of water-based clear finishes that are faulty and not worth much consideration. If the package does not clearly show the vehicle as ACRYLIC RESIN and WATER, then you do not have the furniture finish of the future. The modern paint store scene is changing rapidly and the play on the word "latex" is now predominant, denoting the many water-base mixes now available. Depend upon a reliable dealer and always remember that there are no "bargains" in latex paints, as they can be easily made cheaper and cheaper at the manufacturing level by the mere addition of more and more water.

I recall the first introduction of a latex indoor paint some thirty years ago and how much ridicule and scoffing it had to survive. Now, the latex paints have become the best and most popular paints, eliminating the human toxicity, the fire hazard, and the very dangerous lead, which is being replaced with zinc.

The best acrylic-latex clear varnish that I've found on the market is made by Sears-Roebuck. Their mix performs properly by brushing on easy, drying out within the hour, levels into a smooth surface, and becomes almost scratch-proof. I know of other good brands, but they are presently supplied only to industry. If you follow directions on the Sears can carefully, you will create a velvety surface as smooth as crystal glass and even smoother than professionals produce with sprayed-on lacquers. The result is a silken semigloss that can be dulled down, if you wish, with a piece of crocus cloth, or left as is and highlighted into the finest finish you have ever seen with a rubdown of hard carnauba paste wax. On the face of the container it clearly states: INTERIOR LATEX, CLEAR SATIN FINISH VARNISH.

There are other clear water-base varnishes being introduced, but make certain they show acrylic resin in the vehicle report rather than alkyd resin. I've found the alkyd resin types of clear varnishes to be most unsatisfactory; they take many hours to dry out and they set up a soft, undesirable finish.

If you are refinishing a hardwood article with this new acrylic-latex clear varnish, such as maple, cherry or walnut, two applications should be enough, each drying within the hour, so that your chair or table will be ready for use again within two hours. On the softer or more porous woods, you

may want three or four coatings, all quickly and easily applied without odor. Obviously, there is little dust problem
with a finish that dries so quickly and if accidental scratches
should occur later on, they can be quickly repaired with a
touch-up. They are very thin finishes, but will wear and
wear.

Finally, there are now excellent water-base epoxy-latex
finishes on the market that are superior in many ways to the
usual oil floor and deck paints or enamels. They apply easily
and dry out smooth and quickly and they will withstand
extremely hard wear, indoors or outdoors. No matter what
the protective coating need is now, it can be solved without
the need of the toxic oil paint and finishes. The refinisher's
future is now completely guaranteed through safe, sane, and
sensible options.

The urethane or polyurethane clear finishes have been improved and probably will not lift off in a plastic sheet as they
sometimes did in the past. The promotion behind this type
of finish is powerful and many refinishers use them, but I
still find that the tung oil varnishes, brush-on or wipe-on,
are much more durable and impervious to damage, such as
scratching. Tung oil, by the way does not come from an oil
well. It comes from a tree. As of this date, I would prefer to
follow the tung-oil route or the new acrylic-latex route. But,
the choices are all yours.

A REFRESHER COURSE

Here are the questions that beginners ask most often about refinishing antiques and the answers to them. For many readers, the questions will anticipate those in their minds; for other readers, this question-and-answer section should serve as a short refresher course in avoiding the common pitfalls of refinishing.

QUESTION: Is the value of antique furniture damaged when you strip off the old finish to restore it?

ANSWER: Absolutely not, if properly done. People have been persuaded otherwise by those who do claim you lower the value of the article. There are thousands of pieces of valuable old-time artglass that remain as bright and gay today as on the days they were blown or molded. There are thousands of beautiful antique houses that have been fixed and restored more than once. There are thousands of so-called antique automobiles that look good and run well, sometimes even better, after being mauled and overhauled. Why, then, should antique furniture have to remain shoddy and in various states of non-use? Just as a connoisseur of the fine arts would take great care in restoring his valuable paintings and vases, so you, too, should treat your valuables likewise and refinish them as best as you can, having no fear of any decrease in value if restored properly. The chances are that the value of your collection will only rise. Useable and unmaimed antiques are the best ones. Antiquity does not have to become a part of broken-down obsolescence.

QUESTION: Why is it that antiques dealers do not restore their wares?

ANSWER: It is not because the values of their merchandise would decline. Dealers are in the business of buying and selling "as is," and this is the wiser way for them to keep pricing lower. Secondly, and more importantly, the dealer would not know what kind of color, hue, or finish you would prefer. You might like one of his tables for size and shape, but if he had refinished it in a reddish tone you might bypass the opportunity and the higher cost. It is much better that you do exactly what you want done for your home.

QUESTION: Why do some people claim that paint removers will destroy or remove that nice old patina?

ANSWER: What do they think patina is, anyway? True patina is only the aged coloration of the wood itself and not the finish that man applied. The persons that are so often concerned about patina are most often referring to the old finish which may be shellac or varnish with bacon fat, hair grease, and human sweat ground in. If one prefers to believe that the patina is the smooth and worn-looking shading of the old finish, be assured that you can duplicate any semblance of that finish in your own shop. There isn't any paint remover of the type that has been recommended in this book that will remove patina.

QUESTION: Does the worn-looking finish, often called patina, indicate true antiquity?

ANSWER: Not necessarily. Not even the aged-looking finish or wood appearance. Any surface appearance can be duplicated quite handily and the wood itself can be treated to make that last-century complexion. I have matched fifty-year-old pine to two-hundred-year-old pine. Do not let "patina" confound you. In the main it is a nice sounding professional like word that often covers up ignorance. Refinish in a way that is most pleasing to your own eyes, judging the best possible color blending to whatever you have planned for the mood of a room.

QUESTION: Why is it better to strip furniture with a commercial liquid-solvent type of paint remover rather than a sharp metal blade or a piece of broken glass?

ANSWER: The scraping process will cost you many extra hours of labor and may also cost you a trip to the surgeon. The advice on scraping is pure unadulterated folly. Scrape-off zealots are not only wasting time but they are also ruining the original wood surfaces forever. Obviously, as they scratch off the old finish they also scratch off some of the valuable wood and change the shape of things to come.

QUESTION: Why do some advise against the use of the quicker and cleaner water-wash paint remover?

ANSWER: Probably because they simply just don't believe in changing a method that has worked for them in the past. There is no old furniture that cannot withstand a quick water-washing, particularly as such older woods have been somewhat saturated with oil stains, oil fillers, oil finishes, and oily polishes. A water-wash might occasionally lift a piece of veneering that was about to fall off anyway, as all old veneering was done with glues that were not waterproof. You can quickly correct this rare occurrence with the improved, quick-setting waterproof glues. I have knowledge firsthand of thousands of furniture-stripping operations and can promise you that the water-washing removers are much better to use, providing they are really water-wash and not just water-rinse. Read the product labels carefully.

QUESTION: Does the water-washing stripping method raise the grain of the wood and is this condition serious or very objectionable?

ANSWER: Sometimes the wood grain will rise again, but this is not an important condition or objection. It will be quickly corrected during the initial stages of the refinishing process, and you will not forget to lightly buff with steel wool after sealing in the new stain. All the "whiskers" will be shaved right off! Raised grain should be a minor worry. The wood grain story has been blown out of all rightful proportion. Good cabinetmakers have always washed their new woods with water, deliberately raising as much grain as possible to assure a perfectly smooth surface in the end. The time it will take to buff off some raised grain is about one-fiftieth of the time wasted in scraping off old paint remover sludge.

QUESTION: As I collect furniture, how often will it be necessary to use paint remover and strip away old finishes?

ANSWER: A rule of thumb is that when you are reclaiming old furniture, you will have to remove the old finish at least fifty percent of the time. Paint removing or stripping is not always an essential part of the answer to restoration. First, try the cleaning, rubbing, and polishing way. The old finish may perform well enough for another generation.

QUESTION: In the event that I cannot use a paint remover because of allergy or smell, or do not have the facilities, what then?

ANSWER: Give all of your paint removal problems to a local professional paint stripper. There are many that offer this service, most of whom can be located in the yellow pages of your telephone book. They can do quick and excellent work at modest costs to you, leaving all of the neater decorating work for yourself. These services are sound propositions when you figure what you might have spent on gloves, paint remover, and cleaner. I would question some of the present rumors about these shops. Someone may tell you not to use them because they "tank dip." Keep this in mind: the old tank-dipping process of years ago was nothing more than ruinous hot water and caustic lye. The old-time tank dip was good enough for articles like solid wood doors and shutters, and probably some heavier solid pine articles, but devastating to veneered pieces and furniture made of mahogany, walnut, maple, and certain softer whitewoods. Definitely, the old-time tank dipper ruined about everything that could be called "parlor" furniture. The modern shop may still have a hot tank for stripping solid woods and rougher pieces, but the operator should know best and will very likely strip your finer pieces with solvent-type paint removers, not much differently than you would at home. When you have a quality piece of furniture, consult with the professional stripper first to make sure it will not be soaked in any caustic or hot dip.

QUESTION: Why do you recommend a slightly thinned-down quality furniture varnish and not lacquer, shellac, or the synthetics in the vinyl or urethane class?

ANSWER: Good furniture varnish will not dry out like lacquer and shellac, which will become brittle and scratchy as time wears on. And the varnishes are more predictable and durable than the newer vinyls or urethanes. I once restored a large desk and tried one of the new synthetics. It looked beautiful. However, some days later an accidental nick appeared at the edge of the worktop. Air got underneath the plastic and all of the finish could be pulled off in a sheet. Urethanes or polyurethanes have been improved considerably since then, but why not stay with the varnish that has done so well for so many years? Lacquers cannot be successfully brushed on. They dry and set up too quickly. If you had a spray booth and lacquer spraying guns and nozzles that cost upward to two thousand dollars, then you could apply modern lacquers. Penetrating wood sealer and finish may be wisely used at times, but I use them only when working on raw wood and when I want a pigmented color scheme quickly. The wood sealer-and-finish mixes are durable like the recommended type of varnish. Shellac, as most everyone knows, will not stand up to party drinks or water.

Also, do not forget the white ring problem that you will eliminate with the quality varnish. Hopefully, the varnish that you use will contain a tough resin called tung oil or alkyd. Again, read the package labels.

QUESTION: Why don't you recommend any oil- or silicone-type of furniture polish?

ANSWER: Wood finishes need protection from wear and a yearly application of a hard carnauba paste wax is the best provider that I know of. Oils may shine for a while, but the oils do not build up any protective wall. Eventually, the oils or silicones are taken away by evaporation or by your hands and your clothing. "Oil feeding" is pure poppycock, unless the oil applications are made on unfinished woods for outdoor furniture. Oils and silicones are remarkable dust collectors, regardless of the odor of lemon, orange, or banana.

QUESTION: What are the characteristics of the prepared wood stains?

ANSWER: Most wood stain color lines are excellent if sold under established brand names, but always remember that a "Danish Wheat" on a piece of maple wood may become an "Italian Rye" on a piece of softer pine wood. On raw woods, always make sure to apply the mix of shellac and alchohol before applying the stain. The heavier dose of stain the more color, but also the less chance of showing off beautiful wood graining. Keep the color pigmentation at lower levels by thinning down the stain with paint thinner, which is mineral spirits. Sometimes, however, you may have to make the heaviest possible pigmentation to cover up inferior wood blemishes or imperfections.

QUESTION: What do people mean when they talk about "refractory" paint?

ANSWER: Refractory means obstinate, and as most of the old-time paints are very difficult to remove, the word refractory became known as a type of paint. Refractory paint is the old-time milk paint, really made of milk, lime, oil, and color. Some of these paints have served farm buildings for as long as fifty years, while modern commercial paints might not do as well for eight years. The best attempt to equal the old milk or refractory paints is the development of the present-day acrylic water emulsion paints. The latex paints for indoor work are substantial improvements over the old. All are water-emulsible types and this book will tell you the best types of remover to use when stripping.

QUESTION: Is it true that there aren't any "original" pieces of furniture available in the shops or at auctions?

ANSWER: Yes, but there are exceptions. It is possible that an original from a famous cabinetmaker still lies hidden in a barn or attic, but where? And, who would know for sure? Every piece of furniture that is available to us has been re-produced, and, if carefully and faithfully made should be good enough for us. There are originals of another nature, of course. Your grandfather may have made a chair or table and that is an original. You may find originals that were made by lesser-known cabinetmakers, constructed yesterday or within the past one hundred years. You may also find originals from factories that were producing first-class work as late as the early twentieth century. Originals of Chippendale, Sheraton, Adams, Duncan Phyfe, Hepplewhite, made by the better cabinetmakers of more than one hundred years ago, are carefully guarded.

QUESTION: Do I have to seek out true old antiques if I want the styles of the old cabinetmakers?

ANSWER: No. Most furniture made since early times and to this day reflects in many ways the designing of the old and famous cabinetmakers. A true antique is presumed to be over one hundred years old and the real age of any piece of furniture can become a guessing game for all concerned. The article may be auctioned off from an 1800 homestead, but that does not in any way guarantee that the article is as old. It may be only thirty years old, but old-looking from hard wear. Primarily, look for styles and designs that please you most, keeping in mind quality workmanship. Much of today's contemporary or traditional furniture copies from the Early American, Empire, Federal, and even Victorian periods. The choice is yours. Mixing old and new will provide you with a broader and more flexible base.

QUESTION: Would it be wiser to buy a broken, warped, and cracked reproduction or a later reproduction in reasonably good condition?

ANSWER: I would take the newer reproduction. You are in the business of furnishing a firm foundation for your family and it is always better to leave the haggling about the value of the past to the professionals. Give the experts the problems of neglect and misuse and do not forget that many of the old cabinetmakers were not good at their trade. Old does not always signify good.

UNDERSTANDING THE FURNITURE YOU COLLECT AND RESTORE

A serious collector of antique furniture should never lose the urge for excellence when filling vacant spots in the home with well-preserved and distinctive possessions, both old and new. One does not have to become an "antiquer," but, assuredly, the older patterns and craft cannot be discounted or crossed off one's list, as they are the prototypes of most all present-day furnishings. In addition to the pleasures of reclamation and acquisition, a basic knowledge of the origins of furniture styles can make an important contribution toward the relationship and the worth of your tangible assets.

After studying scores of records and books on furniture, I have concluded that chair styles invariably set the drift of a cabinetmaker's mind. The subject of chairs alone could not be covered in one hundred large volumes because there are thousands of different chairs.

When I set out to learn to recognize furniture styles, I soon found myself inundated in an overwhelming heavy stream of a very intricate and complex industry. The thought of being able to identify the thousands of cabinetmakers' whimsies was cast overboard. It did not take long to realize that one must follow a system of orderly reduction and deduction to achieve recall, holding one's aim on only general spans of styling. Otherwise, one will be caught in a network of contouring and patterning by way of turnings, slats, and spindles. The age-old craft of locking pieces of shaped wood together in order to provide human comforts in style was not to be dispelled, and I gradually unwound the tangles with an uncomplicated plan that produces reasonable surety of identification most every time.

There is no single authority that I know of who has absorbed this mammoth and complex subject. One very well known and ambitious writer exhausted more than 1,500 book pages to explain some of his favored Puritan style of furniture. Another annotator published at least six tomes to outline his history of American antique furniture. It is apparent that furniture students and historians have, at some time, become burdened with the enormous number of different ways that wood has been framed to give man his rest. Since the 1600s, more than thirty basic furniture styles were charted and made in the Western Hemisphere.

No one knows when the first chair was constructed or "invented," but it seems natural to believe that man has searched for a more comforting sitting place since the day he found the way to stand and walk on two feet. Thousands of good and bad furniture makers have come and gone and it is also reasonable to believe that each one of them claimed the right to self-expression through a piece of wood. Therefore, to help lighten the load and to keep your learning on the level of a practical, energizing, and profitable pastime, I have summarized the history of furniture making so that you will be able to escape from the labyrinth of what I first called "the real wilderness of the woods."

The first step is sifting out the names of the classic styles that have primarily set the designing trends of the trade for three hundred years. The second step is to group all the titles of American innovations and, bit by bit, chip away the extravagant and endless repetitious detail that causes the confusion. Finally, the overstuffed monster will be thinned down to a practical size, through a few effective clues that turn folly into fact.

This simplified list combines only the names of some famous people that were caught up in the world of furniture making and the more important names given as American periods. All of the styles that were introduced to create the American "fad" periods are still in popular use and being reproduced daily. The dates in this list stand only for origin and length of maximum popularity.

Classifications of American-Made Furniture

Style, Period, or Span	Peak Years
Early American	1607–1790
Queen Anne	1702–1750
Chippendale	1748–1800
Hepplewhite	1770–1830
Sheraton	1790–1850
Duncan Phyfe	1790–1850
Federal	1790–1865
Victorian	1840–1910
Grand Rapids	1860–1920
Modern	1920–

By studying these ten general categories, you will mastermind most every woody curve, slope, slant, and angle, residual of carefully cultivated piles of shavings and sawdust. It is the main trunk of the tree that concerns us, not the twiggy terms like Colonial, Carver, Brewster, Puritan, Pilgrim, Primitive, Eastlake, Shaker, Pennsylvania Dutch, Greek Revival, Empire, Regency, Jacobean, et cetera.

Early Yankee craftsmen were observing opportunists, innovating and copying every conception from around the globe, and willing to chance mixes of designs in the hope of a direct hit and greater profit. EARLY AMERICAN suitably covers it all in our refining and reducing process.

QUEEN ANNE is a popular style of furniture to this day, frequently being copied in whole or in part. The style was named for Queen Anne, ruler of England from 1702 to 1714. She was the sister of Mary, the prior queen and wife of William, known together as William and Mary. William was a Dutchman and the Queen Anne style was conceived by the Dutch. The style was so attractive and appealing that many cabinetmakers in England and in America adopted it for their own and have produced so much of it that practically every home has one article that could be called Queen Anne. The Dutch do get credit for the ornamental cabriole or arched legs and "pad" feet, but the accompanying shell, fan, or leafy sculpturing originated in China, as evidenced in the old books of Chinese art.

CHIPPENDALE. Thomas Chippendale operated a furniture making shop in London, England, from about 1748 to 1780. He created a new fad in furniture by using the straight and square leg and he also adopted broad-shouldered, square-type chair backs. His marketing influence was strong and, although he pushed Queen Anne to one side for a while, he finally added a slight variance of the Queen Anne legs to some of his chairs. You can learn the identity of Chippendale mainly through his chair backs and not the legs. (Some claim he was the first to use the ball and claw foot.) The Chippendale style became very popular in America and many American cabinetmakers turned out better Chippendale than Chippendale himself. In fact, it is reported that the very best Chippendale was made by John Goddard, an early American cabinetmaker in Rhode Island.

HEPPLEWHITE. George Hepplewhite was also a famous

furniture stylist. For some years he competed against Chippendale for highest honors, actively conducting his London, England, shop from about 1760 to 1790. He started the idea of inside curves to chair backs and is most famous for the "shield back" chair style, quantities of which are still being made in part or in whole. Hepplewhite used much of the Queen Anne styling also, but he did not like Chippendale's straight and square leg, so he tapered it and often decorated it.

SHERATON. Thomas Sheraton was not a cabinetmaker. He was to make his living and fame by selling designs, operating out of London, England, from about 1790 to 1830. It is said that American cabinetmakers adopted some of his styling before the English cabinetmakers, turning out very rectangular backs to chairs that Sheraton copied from the French. Sheraton dared to go Hepplewhite one step further by tapering down Chippendale's leg still more and almost to a pointed foot. Many of his leg fashions were "fluted," and that was his sole "invention."

DUNCAN PHYFE was Scotch-born but operated his most successful shop in downtown Manhattan, New York, from about 1790 to 1840. Several wealthy families bought his work and the news spread rapidly, making a Duncan Phyfe production popular. Another "fad" took hold! Phyfe became the most famous American cabinetmaker, but do not forget that there have been hundreds of very skillful cabinet shops in our new land. Phyfe "invented" the slightly concaved-curved legs and arms, almost directly in opposition to the convex curved legs of Federal design, as you will see later. Phyfe's design was of a much heavier nature than his predecessors' work, probably leading us into the chunkier styles of Victorian and Grand Rapids. His chair backs were artistically designed, not very remote from the French or Sheraton designs.

FEDERAL is the result of tinkering and tampering with Sheraton or French designing, but of a less classical and heavier nature. Legs were sculptured and fluted and most often the edgings on chairs, stands, and sofas were ornamented in wood. I believe that the surface indentations and the straight-line heftiness is the key to most Federal production, much of which is still being copied. Empire, which is basically French, was the template for Federal and therefore not a unique style.

VICTORIAN includes many prior styles and exists successfully to this day. It incorporates alterations to all the classic designs that we have outlined, one good example being the legs and the feet which could remind one of the Queen Anne cabriole legs and duck feet, but blunted or shaved down. Victorian, overall, is very sturdy and chunkier than Federal or Duncan Phyfe. It seems that, as the American furniture making industry grew older during the nineteenth century, all production became heavier or thicker. (Was it then that Americans got the notion that quantity was true value?) Spool construction is Victorian. Overstuffed chairs and sofas with curved or medallion center frames are Victorian. The prime expressions of Victorian can be summed up through ornateness, circular designing, spool turnings, solidness, and thickly stuffed chair seats and sofas. Much of it could be called handsome. Most of it is very durably constructed.

GRAND RAPIDS became the winner in the race to sell the most furniture by weight. It was all mass-produced by machine and was largely marketed through the fast-growing mail-order houses. At long last, even the poorest farmer could supply a sturdy resting place for every member of his family. The vision that returns to me when Grand Rapids is mentioned is that of shaped and smoothed cordwood for the strongest elephantine seat. It seems that the contention of most value in furniture through weight and quantity of wood sprouted during the Federal era and came into full bloom after the Civil War, when American woodlands were being ruthlessly mutilated. At the beginning of this century, a two-hundred-pound Grand Rapids table was offered for $9, while a one hundred and twenty-five pounder sold for $6! Old mail-order catalogs indicate weight to be very important in selling furniture and it is my opinion that the various Grand Rapids factories, not all in Michigan, were allied to the savage lumbering business. As a rule, the wood was oak that was heavily varnished, or veneered tops with cheaper wood as filler. Durability could be fully guaranteed, but not design in class. Grand Rapids must have given support with some tolerance of comfort to millions of tired working people. Chair seats were thinly padded and covered with molded fiber or leather. Sometimes there was painted striping added for glamour at slightly higher prices. Mission style competed in this category, under our plan of refining and reduction. Mission was almost as heavy looking in a boxlike structuring, being without arches, curves, and ornamentation. Grand Rapids is good for wear and hard service.

MODERN is a reproduction of most all the strains of the older classics, sold as Traditional or Contemporary styling. In this classification, we note "butcher block" creeping into the market to keep the boxlike structuring of Mission and the weight contest alive. There are some factories that carefully reproduce in good quality classic styles and there are individual cabinetmakers that imitate with excellence, if not better than some of the old shops that did not have the benefits of modern tools and power. Modern is not antique, but much of it copies antiquity.

The classical and nonclassical productions since the 1600s has been commonly separated by calling it "parlor" or "country" respectively, but all of it is the result of intermarriage and crossbreeding, over and over. Hundreds of woodcrafters made use of parts of every old popular idea and created thousands of varied combinations. Every piece of furniture that is available to us is a hybrid, in some way. There is no absolute purity, but you might be the lucky person to possess a true original that was made by some well-known cabinetmaker in the dim past, being the owner of a piece of structured wood worth more than fifty thousand dollars.

Keep in mind that our Early American makers were busy long before the four named famous cabinetmakers were born. The early Yankees created many useful ideas on their own, although some of the results clearly show an underdevelopment of skill, crude workmanship, and equipment. I think principally of the primitive Pilgrim and Puritan spans, from which some uncomfortable-looking structures came, like certain chairs and stands that seem to be held together with frozen strings of sausage or bologna. However, many of these pieces bear out true antiquity and are very valuable. Expert woodcrafting arrived in the latter 1600s. The Queen Anne styling was being produced in America before William and Mary named it Queen Anne. The very best of Chippendale came from Rhode Island and the best of Hepplewhite came from Maryland. Early American is mostly desirable being mixed by Yankee ingenuity and some free thinking. Early American is a friendly species that is easy to housebreak. The popularity of some American innovations is worldwide and honor must be paid to our colonial workmen. Who would ignore the charm of butterfly tables in hard maple? Is there a better-looking sewing cabinet than the Martha Washington? What types of chairs can be found more adaptable and useful than the Windsors, or the many variations of the ladder or slat backs? Early American also included the colorful Hitchcock chair, the sleekness of fine Shaker workmanship, the beautiful Pennsylvania Dutch designing and coloring and the distinguished Boston or Salem rocking chair. As a final salute to pure Americana, what elder could forget the famous Victorian Morris chair that has sired the present-day popular loungers and recliners? Standing alone, Early American styling and workmanship is varied enough and good enough to adequately equip any castle or home. May the memory linger on.

The following sketches will provide some proof of the cleverness of Early American furniture makers. The rocking cradle may have first appeared in northwestern Europe, but it took a colonial lad on the west shore of the Atlantic to originate the rocking chair. Experts are uncertain whether the very first rocking chair was put together in the Boston area or in the Philadelphia area, but the Boston or Salem rocker did enjoy wide fame first. The Boston or Salem rocker is characteristically finished in satiny black and carries some colored stenciling. Good reproductions have always been made. There are other good rocking chairs of American origination, such as the Lincoln, the platform, the wicker, and the bentwood creations. The Windsor bow-back armchair is only one of the scores of variations of Windsor. Any chair with a spindled back in an up-and-down arrangement is Windsor, including the popular captain's chairs.

The following twelve outlines adequately display the outcome of our distillation program. Study these illustrations and your judgment will be reasonably accurate in classifying the changes wrought over a three-hundred-year span.

AMERICAN FURNITURE:
A GUIDE TO STYLES

AMERICAN ORIGIN CLASSICS

Slat Back

Windsor

Boston Rocker

Victorian

This first grouping of four chairs are placed together for three reasons. First, they are the result of pure American inventiveness in cabinetmaking. Second, they are in popular use to this day, not only in our country but all over the world. Third, they indicate the drift from complete handcrafted work to the heavier mass-machined work, comparing the slat back and Windsor to the Victorian.

Note the similarity of the nineteen-century Victorian that was adaptable to machine work, to the much earlier hand-crafted Queen Anne on the following page. Always keep in mind that any chair with slats running horizontally across the back, whether two slats or more and regardless of the shape of the slats, is slat back. Every chair or bench, such as a deacon's bench, with up-and-down spindles for the back construction, is Windsor style.

By knowing these four distinctive styles and the following eight, you will appreciate practically every line and curve that has been contributed toward making a piece of furniture, stick by stick.

ENGLISH ORIGIN CLASSICS

Chippendale

Hepplewhite

Queen Anne

Sheraton

ENGLISH ORIGIN CLASSICS

This second grouping of four chairs ties together the very finest of handcraft in cabinetmaking, long before the machine mass production age. The design for these chairs did not originate in America, but American cabinetmakers produced great quantities of these styles, and in some instances popularized them before the English cabinetmakers. The styles seem to be everlasting and are reproduced to this day in various "married" forms.

It is quite easy to differentiate between Queen Anne, Chippendale, Hepplewhite, and Sheraton if you will remember that any Queen Anne invariably carries the cabriole leg and various options of the duck foot style. Chippendale backs may have many designs incorporated inside the frame of the back, which is always round-shouldered. Hepplewhite is always a full design back without framing, mostly in the shield motif, while Sheraton backs are rectangular backs.

The legs of Chippendale, Hepplewhite, and Sheraton will vary, as they sometimes take on the ball and claw or even the Queen Anne style. Go by the backs! Sometimes by the legs! It is the shape of chairs that has been my best guide in identifying furniture, and that is not "sitting bull."

AMERICAN 1800S HEFTIES

Duncan Phyfe

Federal

Grand Rapids

Mission

AMERICAN 1800S HEFTIES

Although Duncan Phyfe is considered to be the most famous cabinetmaker in America, his production is heavier and is often mistaken for Federal, because the only outstanding difference in many instances is the inside curve of the Phyfe leg and the outside curve of the Federal leg. Also, Federal is generally heftier, much of it coming out of the machine age. Basically, these four chairs have been grouped together to show the trend into the machine age with less and less handcraft, plus the need of more and more furniture at lower and lower prices to meet the need of the workingman's pocketbook.

Grand Rapids stands quite alone. It is all very chunky and heavy but has some shaping where a machine could do it. It is practical and useful and there are quantities of it sold as "antiques" in this modern age.

Mission is practically all angular and can be all machined; no real cabinetmaking skills are required. Mission is not very popular, except in some Western areas where Mission first took hold from Spanish inclinations. The present-day butcher-block construction harks back to Mission style. True originality in cabinetmaking ended about one hundred and fifty years ago.

Queen Anne   *Chippendale*   *Hepplewhite*   *Sheraton*

Phyfe   *Federal*   *Victorian*   *Grand Rapids*

All Early American

TABLES, STANDS, SIDEPIECES

The clue to determining the furniture period is found in the legs and feet, the same process of deduction that was recommended for identifying chairs. The following sketches of legs will provide you with the same easy memory system of learning popular basic styles. In order to carry out the refinement to legs and feet, it was necessary to make one exception by showing two of Chippendale's legs, as against a single leg each for Queen Anne, Hepplewhite, Sheraton, and Phyfe. This is not partiality; it is because Chippendale switched from the square leg that he started off with to a cabriole leg and ball and claw foot that would better carry him into the circle of stylists. All of the designated styles represent the beginning of the cabinetmaking eras and, of course, there have been numerous deviations created since by thousands of craftmen, both good and bad.

The Queen Anne leg-and-foot style seems to have remained intact with purity. It is a real classic and has continued to be popular. Chippendale's square leg is still used, probably for economics in this machine age, while there are many variations of his ball and claw foot connected to a broad cabriole leg. The square, but tapered, leg of Hepplewhite's has held up well and firm. The Sheraton round-tapered leg is probably the most exquisite in the lineup. Duncan Phyfe and his Federal competitors copied extensively, but Phyfe won the race with the most fame through the use of his concaved leg, fluted or not. Victorian carries all the influences of prior years that could be inexpensively made by machine. Grand Rapids is wood tonnage in oak, while Mission is all squared pieces and not distinctive at all.

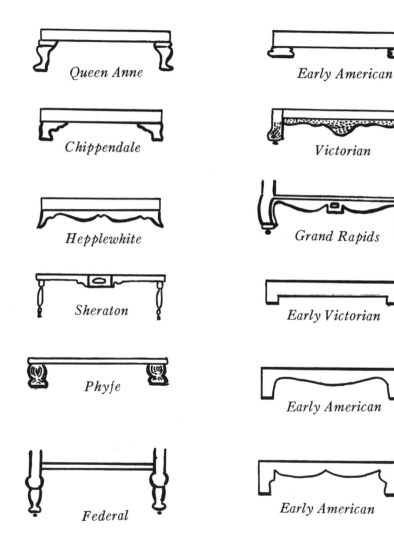

Queen Anne

Early American

Chippendale

Victorian

Hepplewhite

Grand Rapids

Sheraton

Early Victorian

Phyfe

Early American

Federal

Early American

CHESTS OF DRAWERS, COMMODES, DESKS, BUREAUS

In the identification of these antiques, one need not consider the many variations of the sides—such as bowed, bombé, or serpentine—unless it is to be pinpointed to a provincial cabinet-making group like the Pennsylvania Dutch. If any of the classic styles were copied, then the easiest identification is found in the base, which may be called skirt or foot.

The following sketches will provide you with the basic differences. Many of the most popular styles found today are nothing more than scrolled pieces of wood with many variables that combine both base and feet, and that is copying really true Early American.

BEDS

Beds were first made during the early eighteenth century. As to detecting style, take note of the posts, footboarding, or headboarding. If the posts are of the main concern, refer to the sketches on table legs. Posts that are topped with pineapples, urns, cones, or balls are from early American influences. Beds without posts may be very modern, like the Hollywood bed, but many attractive old beds have distinctive head and foot cabinetmaking makeups. The spool bed is one example. If the head and foot remind you of the two sides of a lyre, that could be a Phyfe or Federal favorite. Very Early American have high bed posts that were used for canopies and side curtains, when body heat was the only source of warmth. Brass and iron beds were very popular within this past century and have become collector's items. Bed history, as it has been written by many historians, is comparatively vague and brief. Prior to the eighteenth century, beds were strung together with rope or rawhide and prior to the canopies and curtains, beds were completely paneled in to keep the cold out, reminding one of sleeping inside of a box.

By all means, the best bed is the one that will help you sleep comfortably and that depends upon the nature of the mattresses and springs that cannot be credited to the cabinet or furniture makers.

UPHOLSTERED FURNITURE

If the chair, sofa, or loveseat has exposed framework, it can be put into a period class. Heavily stuffed chairs that are commonly known as Wingback, Club, Cogswell, or Martha Washington will often have open wooden leg work and reflect the style that was copied. As to loveseats and sofas, both the legwork and the framework of the back and the sides, if they are exposed, will come into play. The back may readily show the original creativeness of an old master, not much differently than the backs of Hepplewhite or Sheraton chairs, or the back may represent the Federal or Victorian period.

Federal generally shows heavy stretchers with corresponding heavy arched sides, plus fat leg and foot work. Phyfe's preferences would dictate the lyre design at the sides, plus his typical concaved and arched legs. Victorian is grooved framework that is wavy or circular, with additional sculpturing or carving in the form of curled leaves and clusters of grapes. The backs of Victorian sofas or loveseats, in particular, form three sections, the middle section being a medallion with carved work at the top.

ANTIQUE FURNITURE OR ANTIQUE STYLE FURNITURE?

There may be no appreciable difference in the general appearance of a true antique made over one hundred years ago and a faithful reproduction that was made twenty years ago. In fact, many people might not find the differences under any circumstances and that is not bad, as we primarily search for compatibility of style and soundness of construction. A friend recently said to me, "I don't like antiques," and I was surprised to learn that he carried a misconception for so many years. My friend's home is somewhat larger than the average American home and it contains a bounty of very beautiful antiques. His acquisitions are an accumulation of four generations, through inheritances, all quality-crafted and well preserved from footstool to bedstead. Apparently, the word "antique" disturbs some minds by creating false and uncomfortable scenes of rot, decay, and collapsing, rickety junk. Or, perhaps the word "antique" suggests squared tree limbs along the Grand Rapids line, or it may create the image of warped worthlessness from an old chicken roost that was cleaned up and re-nailed for a settee. Take heed, the sole difference many times between "antique" and "antique style" is the number of years of age. Always remember that all available furniture, whether made today or yesteryear will carry some part of a style born of antiquity, with curves or angles going backward for several hundred years. Set your heart on the styles that you like best. If you are lucky to obtain a real antique for a bargain, so much the better, but do not sacrifice the rest of the home by spending too much for that one "original."

KEEP IT SIMPLE

Throughout this furniture distilling process, many conflicting terms were discarded, such as William and Mary, Adam, Colonial, Puritan, Primitive, and Empire. As one example, Empire was not included as it was never popular in America. It was a massive style, dictated by Napoleon, and, it was sufficiently expressed during the Phyfe and Federal working periods. There are hundreds of volumes on furniture and, if you delve into them, you too can find thousands of conflicting sketches, photographs, and descriptions. That is why this easy and simplified system of basic information for obtainable and available furniture was created.

Shaker
Dining Chair

Southern
Style Bench
and Chest

Tip Top
Table

Sheraton
Lamp Stand

CONVERSATION OR CONSERVATION FURNITURE

Many finely crafted antiques are still alive and healthy but most of them that are genuine will come into the market slowly, and in small lots. There are thousands of long-line families that are using and preserving these articles, having accumulated them through inheritances from three to ten generations past. Follow the auctions that refer to the dissolving of estates and you will see the uncovering of many real charms, probably for the first time in three hundred years. Dealers will be there and they will set the pace of the bidding. Do not be surprised if a broken-down Queen Anne mahogany table of 1740 vintage goes for several thousand dollars!

The following pictures will give you an idea of the uncommon, unique and still very useful articles. They are the result of careful conservation but you can turn it all around to intriguing conversation. The two slat-back Shaker chair was not sold on the wood tonnage basis. All Shaker is very well constructed and truely American. Originals of Shaker are quite valuable but you can find honestly made reproductions of this twentieth century, at prices that will fit any pocketbook. The small Southern blanket chest and bench has dual uses and this model is well constructed of fine eastern pine. Similar ones can be found at reasonable prices. The small squarish tip-top table in thicker pine is rare in the common market, but they can be found. Notice the long tapered legs on the country pine lamp stand, representing true Sheraton designing. It is a reproduction and not expensive, but may be considered an antique within another generation.

If you cannot afford the real antique, put your sights on the practical and the unusuals that have been well made and that have a good image of the classics. You will be glad that you did!

AFTERWORD

I have presented in the foregoing many of the ways in which you can gain an intelligent understanding of the methods of refinishing furniture. From my years of everyday experience and the more unusual experiences in refinishing with scores of paint removers, stains, clear finishes, as well as various paints of many different brand names, and from firsthand experience in refinishing dozens of pieces of furniture I have developed my own methods. I have been consulted by and have consulted with thousands of people—amateur and professional—who have had refinishing problems to work out. Through the years I have worked closely with both research and development, if those terms describe the ties between the laboratory and market testing of products.

Refinishing and reclaiming old furniture has always given me happy hours. And I know that such a hobby is more fruitful if the refinisher builds on certain basic knowledge. A good plow and an experienced plowhand do not necessarily set the stage for good crops; there must also be good soil. Therefore, a refinisher must have a basic grasp of the hidden values in old pieces of furniture, before it is worthwhile refinishing. That is why I have tried as much as possible to guide you on your way in these lessons on refinishing and reclaiming furniture.

Those who have the best grasp of the common-sense practices are the most certain to have success—and with the least time and money spent, too. It is more and more apparent in business dealings these days that a buyer ought not to be ignorant of the nature of the property he buys. The old maxim, so neatly summed up by the Romans—*Caveat emptor* ("Let the buyer beware")—was never more true.

With knowledge, you may turn this phrase around; the new meaning could be: "Let the seller beware if he is trying to put something over on the intelligent antiquer." And this applies as much to the buying of removers and paints as it does to buying the antiques. Read labels, examine products carefully, and always look over a piece of furniture thoroughly to make sure it is worthy of the work.

Goodbye and good luck!

INDEX